Road Trip to Redemption is a must-read for story of pain, healing, and fighting for your kids' hearts. I was personally challenged and convicted to look beyond superficial, check-mark Christianity. I can't thank Brad enough for empowering me to connect my kids with the real, authentic, life-giving Jesus. I'm looking through my calendar now, booking my own "road trip to redemption."

CHRIS SPRADLIN
Founder of EpicParent.tv
Author of *Sex, Lust & XXX: Fighting for Your Kids' Purity in a Sex-Saturated World*

If you think your family is out of options for reconnecting, whether with your kids or your spouse, this book is for you. *Road Trip to Redemption* is an intimate adventure of one man's journey to recapture the hearts of a family he had all but lost. Filled with practical advice and insight, Brad's vulnerable approach to storytelling kept me turning the pages and opened my heart to the changes I needed to make as a father. What a beautiful story—one that can be everybody's.

ROBERT BEESON
Founder of iShine
Former president and founder of Essential Records

ROAD TRIP
TO REDEMPTION

BRAD MATHIAS

TYNDALE
MOMENTUM

An Imprint of
Tyndale House Publishers, Inc.

Visit Tyndale online at www.tyndale.com.

Visit Tyndale Momentum online at www.tyndalemomentum.com.

TYNDALE is a registered trademark of Tyndale House Publishers, Inc. *Tyndale Momentum* and the Tyndale Momentum logo are trademarks of Tyndale House Publishers, Inc. Tyndale Momentum is an imprint of Tyndale House Publishers, Inc.

Road Trip to Redemption: A Disconnected Family, a Cross-Country Adventure, and an Amazing Journey of Healing and Grace

Published in association with the literary agency of Esther Fedorkevich, Fedd and Company Inc., 606 Flamingo, Austin, TX 78734.

Designed by Beth Sparkman

Edited by Karin Stock Buursma

Library of Congress Cataloging-in-Publication Data

Mathias, Brad.
  Road trip to redemption : a disconnected family, a cross-country adventure, and an amazing journey of healing and grace / Brad Mathias.
    p. cm.
  Includes bibliographical references (p.   ).
  ISBN 978-1-4143-6394-3 (sc)
1. Parent and child—Religious aspects—Christianity. 2. Families—Religious life. 3. United States—Description and travel. 4. Canada—Description and travel. I. Title.
  BV4529.M3675 2013
  277.308'3092—dc23
  [B]   2012038001

Printed in the United States of America

19	18	17	16	15	14	13
7	6	5	4	3	2	1

To my Bethany Rose. Your courage inspires me to be a better father. Your love and trust humble me. I couldn't have asked for a more amazing child to call my own. I love you. Thank you for your patience and persistence in the midst of such pain. I am not worthy even to attempt to capture your spirit on these pages, but by God's grace I have tried.

To my dearest Paige, the most patient wife and mother, who carries great faith for us all. You amaze me still. ☺

To Jessica Elaine. You will always be my "biggest" girl and will always fit in the cradle of my elbow. My elegant intellectual, I shall always admire your thirst for knowledge.

To Caleb, my son. May your heart grow to fit your gifts as I watch from nearby . . . always the proud father.

To my own crazy parents who raised me well despite their frustrations and fears. I love and appreciate the genuine heritage of faith and family you have passed on to me, and now I seek to do the same.

To my community of faith and my dearest comrade, Brian. Strength for the battle and wisdom for the path— I couldn't have made these discoveries without you.

To Robert, my sharp-witted friend for life. You make me a better thinker and writer. Thank you.

To my family at large. Your love and support are immeasurable and precious to me.

To my big brother, "Donk." I love you and am proud to be your little bro.

To Tom Johnson, a genuine man of the faith and one who keeps his word . . . so rare. Thank you for being a mentor worth following.

Unspeakable thanks to my Savior and Lord. I have fought the fight with all my heart, and in my broken state I found your grace. Thank you for not giving up on me, my family, or this generation! Come quickly, Lord Jesus!

Somehow we have overlooked the fact that this treasure called the heart can also be broken, has been broken, and now lies in pieces down under the surface. When it comes to "habits" we cannot quit or patterns we cannot stop, anger that flies out of nowhere, fears we cannot overcome, or weaknesses we hate to admit—much of what troubles us comes out of the broken places in our hearts crying out for relief.

Jesus speaks as if we are all the brokenhearted.
We would do well to trust his perspective on this.

JOHN ELDREDGE, *WAKING THE DEAD:*
THE GLORY OF A HEART FULLY ALIVE

Contents

Foreword

As a close friend and ally to the Mathias family, I was within arm's reach to the story that unfolds in this book. And yet, as I read the story once again, I began to realize the power in the retelling. For if you change the dates and names and some of the circumstances, this could probably be your story. This is likely why you've cracked this book open to begin with. You may be in the first chapters of your personal parenting journey, and the "fog of war" that seems to cloud most days may have you feeling hopeless right now. If so, you will find great comfort as you read these pages, because you will find yourself in them—and with God's providence, you will take away a posture of heart that will lead you to your own story of redemption.

I've known Brad for many years. We're the best of friends, and I know the restoration in his life firsthand. I've also known his beautiful, heroic daughter Bethany since she was a little girl. As you turn these pages, you'll get to know them both, as well as the rest of the family. What you will find here is that God redeems everything he touches, and that redemption is available to all. In reading this book, may that message of hope be transferred to your heart.

Over the next few hours, you're going to nod your head with recognition, laugh, tear up, and experience the exhilaration of the open road. Fasten your seat belt and watch as your heavenly Father makes the signposts clear in your own road trip to redemption.

Brian Hardin,
founder of Daily Audio Bible and author of *Passages*

Introduction

It was January, it was sleeting ice, and it was dark. As I drove across the northern Arizona desert with my dear friend Brian Hardin, we were racing to avoid a serious winter blizzard coming down from the northwest only a few hours behind us.

Driving due east in the high desert at night is a lonely and eerie experience, and that's true without any bad weather to contend with. The seven-thousand-foot average elevation makes for cool evenings any time of year, let alone in the dead of winter. Two-lane, 1960s-era highways are the only option for travel beyond the rutted dirt and gravel switchbacks to the Indian reservations along the way. The high mesas and arroyos make a dark red stain in the distance as the car windows reveal an arid and rocky landscape as far as the eye can see. Of course, not a lick of this was visible at night. Because there were no towns, cities, or gas stations for hundreds of miles, there was also no ground lighting. Instead, we had to drive with only fifty feet or so of dimly illuminated, cracked blacktop in front of us, revealed just long enough for me to keep the SUV we were driving out of the ditch and the boulder-strewn shoulder of the road.

The sleet kept coming. Over the past hour or two, the ice had built to about a solid inch on the roads, and more was being added every minute we drove. The eighteen-wheelers were creeping along at ten miles per hour, and so were we. If the road had been flat, it would just have been slick—somewhat dangerous, but not too bad. But this road was not flat. It was twisty and banked, and it quickly gained and shed elevation every four or five miles as we went up one mesa and down into another valley. The side of the road might have a five-foot drop into a rocky ditch or a five-hundred-foot slide down a cliff face. We just couldn't tell with the conditions outside.

Did I mention there were no real snowplows to speak of? The one salt truck we had seen was no longer going in the same direction we were, returning to its state or county line as we crept farther away from civilization into the looming darkness ahead and the blackest of road ice below.

I hate ice on roads. I can drive through a twelve-thousand-foot mountain pass in the dead of winter with twenty-foot snowbanks on either side and not break a single bead of sweat. In the backcountry of British Columbia, I can navigate old, rutted wilderness-access roads that are absent from the map without slowing at all. But black ice on a two-lane isolated highway in the middle of nowhere is a different matter. That stresses me.

I was tense. I had almost bent the steering wheel in half from the pressure I was exerting on its weakening rubber frame. All this stress came from my fear of losing control while driving at a "reckless" ten to fifteen miles per hour. Rather than risk sliding off the road, I preferred to stop. I wanted to find a hotel with a hot shower, cable TV, and a crummy vending machine that would have Fritos and Coke and a chance to get off this insane highway. Yet I noticed that Brian continued to sit quietly in his seat, absently listening to some eighties rock while chewing on his beef jerky and Corn Nuts. He seemed completely unconcerned about our predicament. I was 110 percent focused on keeping us on the road and out of the ditch, avoiding the semis on both sides of us, and watching diligently for the blizzard that was sure to come up behind us from Utah. Meanwhile, he yawned and stretched out as he took a swig from his water bottle; it seemed he was just about to fall asleep. Either he trusted my driving skills more than I did, or he knew something about the road ahead that I didn't know—or maybe a little of both.

Unpacking the Metaphor

Parenting can be a lot like my evening drive in the desert. As parents, we're doing our best to drive our family safely on unfamiliar highways, far from the comfort of our well-traveled paths. We often encounter unexpected hazardous conditions along the way—bad weather, construction, road detours, and breakdowns. We're constantly engaged in a struggle to keep our vehicles on the road and in between the white lines of life. There are distractions both inside and outside our vehicles all along the way. Out-of-control cars and trucks rush around us, speeding recklessly past or driving dangerously close, and objects in front of us go way too slow. We worry that we missed our exit, and we wonder if we're driving in the right direction or if we've mistakenly gone miles out of our way. We want to get our family safely to our destination, but we're afraid we'll get lost, distracted, or wrecked—or just run out of gas.

As the drivers, we parents can get anxious about everything around us we cannot control. We react by gripping the steering wheel with both hands and squeezing with all our might; we tighten everyone's seat belts and ride the brakes in vain attempts to keep us all safe.

Here's the thing: We can worry with each mile we pass, or we can relax and enjoy the view as we drive by. The truth is, we have a GPS, and we have a map. God has given us his Holy Spirit (GPS) to keep us from getting lost, and we have his Scriptures (map) to show us the way.

We don't have to figure out the best route because we have a navigator already. In fact, we're not even required to steer; God has offered to do that for us too. We really don't have to sweat the details. All we have to do is stay on the road we've been directed to drive on, being careful to avoid hitting any wildlife or falling asleep at the wheel.

If we believe this is true, the "road trip" of parenting becomes an amazing journey of discovery and personal connection, as well as a powerful reminder of the beauty of God's creation around us. Yet if we insist that we alone will chart our course and navigate our lives, we'll miss out on most of the amazing and restful experience God intended. Too often we forget to enjoy the process; we miss the fact that it's a privilege to take the journey at all. If we're not careful, we can become so obsessed with navigating safely from point A to point B that we can't experience anything else but the manic fear of not arriving.

As drivers (parents), we have a choice in it all: We can either react like Brian chose to, in total trust and peace, content to ride along, or we can react the way I did, trying to maintain control and ending up anxious, frustrated, and exhausted the entire way.

* * *

On many levels, I hesitated even to attempt this book, but I felt compelled to share my family's story—of hard lessons learned, battles won and still ongoing—with fellow parents. Our story is told openly and with full transparency, leaving us vulnerable before you. We don't reveal this lightly, but we do it in hopes that it will offer some encouragement to other parents. We all share in the common struggle of being fathers and mothers. Together we're on a parenting pilgrimage, a rite of passage every generation must complete.

This is the story of a family crisis that threatened one of our children. In the aftermath of that crisis, God took me on a profound personal journey, leading me to rethink much of what I thought I knew about being a good father and the goals of Christian parenting. Eventually he directed me to take my family on an extended road trip, and he used that experience—full of incredible natural beauty, hours in the car, and forced family togetherness in a way we hadn't encountered before—to speak to us individually and as a family . . . to bring us healing.

I am not a fan of formulaic how-to books for Christian living. This is not meant to be another three-point version of how to enjoy a better Christian life. I don't wish to give you a false hope of quick resolution to whatever crisis you face. I fear that many parenting books engage little but our need to do *something* to change our circumstances and avoid our pain. That is not this book's purpose. Instead, this book is intended to be an encouragement to any family who finds itself in the midst of a crisis, or to parents feeling a growing concern over the condition of their family. It's specifically for those families who are feeling detached from one another and are looking for ways to reconnect at a heart level. If that sounds familiar, this book is definitely for you.

My hope is for you to be inspired to press on with your calling of being a parent. I want to challenge you not to give up or settle for living in survival mode, and to help you avoid being just another "wounded, weary, and wary" kind of parent.

My goal is to help parents look beyond the external symptoms of their children's behavior to the heart level. Through my story, I want to help you see your kids as they are: multidimensional, unique individuals who need your love and attention, or, simply put, your time. I want to remind you of the difference between kids who appear to be okay and pay lip service to Christianity and those who are genuinely being drawn into their faith by a growing understanding of the overwhelming love God has for them. I want to inspire you to parent out of love and a commitment to gain a deep, lasting connection with your kids, instead of out of debilitating fear and a desperate desire to "get it right." I hope you get a glimpse of what it means to be an authentic parent, even when your past choices—like mine—have not made you the perfect role model.

Throughout the book I've included family photos from our trip so you can experience the ride with us—the ups and downs that made our adventure so memorable. As I tell our family's story, my prayer is that these hard-won insights will be deposited solidly in your mind and heart. The principles my family has discovered have their roots in the Bible and are helpful in every human tragedy and triumph. The truths I've referenced are ancient and remarkable, capable of guiding and directing the most desperate and cynical among us to new hope and life and faith in Christ. The experiences I recount from my own life are intended to encourage everyone to get up and try again, no matter how messy your circumstances or your past.

I believe it will take parents pursuing God diligently and sincerely to change the world, starting in our first missionary field: our own homes. We cannot trust to the efforts of others to educate and engage our own children's hearts to the truth of God and his plan for their lives. We are responsible for keeping our families on the sure road of true life, and we must not be asleep at the wheel. With God as our help, we can overcome dangerous conditions, unfamiliar roads, distractions, and bad weather. May God richly bless you on your own parenting pilgrimage, your own road-trip journey as you seek to lead your family in the most amazing adventure of all.

Peace and grace to you,
Brad Mathias

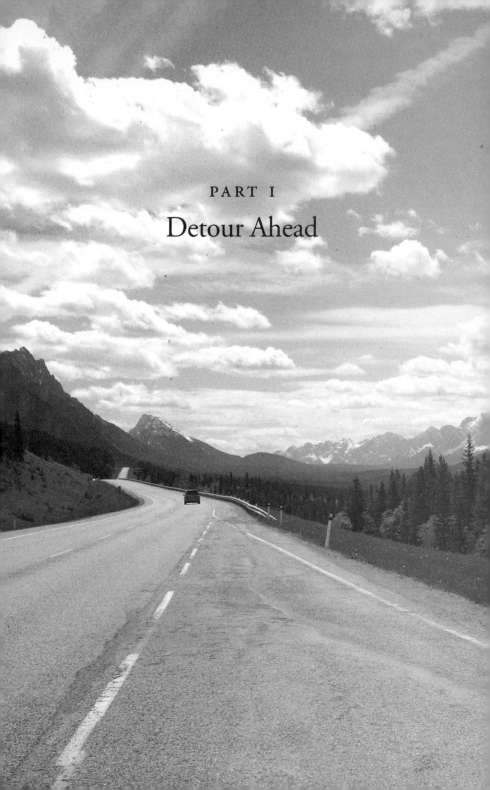

PART I

Detour Ahead

TO HELL AND BACK

I REMEMBER THE PHONE CALL, 2:30 A.M. late in the summer of 2001. I was groggy, disoriented, and alone, lying in the middle of a double bed in a beat-up old hotel on the outskirts of Lake Geneva, Wisconsin.

The phone kept interrupting my fitful sleep, ringing over and over with a harsh and unrelenting insistence. I cursed in the dark as I fumbled for the receiver, reluctant to talk, but willing to do anything to make the noise stop.

As my sleep-fogged mind tried to connect the sounds I was hearing to some slightly functional part of my brain, I could sense more than understand that my wife was yelling angrily at me. She was ranting—no, raving—screaming at times, coldly angry at others. The message was coming through loud and clear: *Don't bother to come home, EVER! Don't call me. Don't ever talk with me again. I am DONE! I am getting an attorney in the morning and filing for divorce.*

I was wide-awake now. A cold pit of nausea formed in my digestive tract. I whispered my question in between her ranting: "But what did I do?"

Of course, I already knew the answer.

I had cheated on her. I had violated our marriage commitment, and worse, I had loved someone else, long before this call disturbed me in the night. That was why I was here in Wisconsin and she was at our place in Iowa with our three children, Jessica, Bethany, and little Caleb. They were six, five, and three years of age, respectively, and they were *the* pride and joy of my life. My marriage . . . well, it seemed it was about to become a testament to one of my greatest disasters and regrets.

Falling in Love and Learning to Pretend

We had married young. Paige and I had come from very different worlds, she a genuine Southern belle of the old Memphis style and I an odd catch from rural Illinois. I was loud and full of confidence, tall and "cute," but not handsome by any stretch. She was short and petite, a gentle soul with beauty, grace, and quiet refinement.

I had pursued her with all I had, with a long-distance dating relationship that would earn me an A for effort and an engagement ring on her hand in eighteen months. We had met when I was a sophomore in my undergraduate studies at Eastern Illinois University and she was a senior at Illinois Wesleyan. We studied hundreds of miles apart but had met at a weekend retreat in Decatur, Illinois, hosted by InterVarsity Christian Fellowship. She went for a weekend of Bible study and fellowship with her fourth-year college classmates, and I went as an indecisive seeker of truth, only casually interested in Christianity, mostly looking to hang with some newfound friends. I was much more curious to find out if InterVarsity girls from other colleges were cuter than the ones I already knew.

I was a lifelong cultural Christian, raised in the severe and legalistic world of a nondenominational association of churches, unorthodox and spiritually abusive. They spoke with authority on all things and believed their particular brand of faith to be the only way to truly experience God. At nineteen years of age, I had been thoroughly overwhelmed by the negativity and harshness of what I thought was Christianity, and I had already developed deep anger and suspicion of the church as a whole. Yet I needed to stay just close enough to it for my own stability, to reduce my well-developed sense of guilt and fear of God's punishment.

Paige had been raised in a blended family, her mother a true Southern lady with deep roots in the traditions of the Bible Belt. She cherished family and faith and had a well-balanced view of the church and mainline denominational observances. Her family members were Methodists and were careful to keep their faith in balance with the realities of normal life. Paige, as a result, had no real baggage with the church or with other Christians, and she trusted her pastor's leading and her family's advice with few reservations.

As I got to know Paige and her family and could see that they were content in their Christian faith, I chose to simply go along with it and not rock the proverbial boat. After all, I was in love, and the movies seem to say that if you're in love, things always work out in the end. But this realization of our different, even conflicting perspectives on faith, life, and spiritual truth led me to avoid revealing myself. I chose instead to adapt and become something both duplicitous and dangerous.

Instead of having an open discussion—an upfront, truthful, and transparent sharing of my reservations about Christianity—I faked it. I was afraid. I believed it was possible that if I told Paige my real feelings about God, church, and faith, I might scare her away.

Looking back, I was in *love*. I was full of adrenaline, hope, and joy at finding someone so beautiful, so kind, and so perfectly suited to balance me. So in my presumption and blinded state, I pushed on, accepting the need to be two people: myself and whoever Paige and her family wanted me to be. I blended in. I accepted and absorbed whatever they seemed to prefer and hid my true self somewhere deep, dark, and far away.

This accommodation of living in two worlds would become my normal, functional state for the next seven years. Not a great foundation to build a life on, let alone a family.

Seven-Year Heartache

In June 1991, Paige and I were married. It turned out to be a memorable day for everyone—a beautiful ceremony and reception, bookended by an outbreak of severe thunderstorms, oppressive humidity, and tornadoes that hit the city of Springfield, Illinois. That was the backdrop on the day we professed our love and vowed before God to become man and wife.

Of course we had an outdoor evening reception, but the rain and wind that battered our tent only seemed to give our festivities some character. Paige and I were young, in love, and full of life. So what if it rained on our wedding day? We didn't care. Nothing could keep us from being husband and wife forever, and we were confident in the future we could create together.

By the end of my graduate studies two years later, Paige and I had gotten used to sharing our single-room studio apartment in downtown Davenport, Iowa. I had learned more about accommodating her needs and wants and had further enhanced my skill at burying my own feelings and frustrations, so we didn't really fight or disagree very often. We each just chose to avoid confrontation and trusted that, sooner or later, the other person would change. Our long-distance romance had settled into a real-life coexistence that centered on my medical studies and her teaching English as a second language at an adult education facility nearby.

We avoided real discussions on faith, family, and personal beliefs. Instead we focused on our goals, our dreams, and our hopes to have children, a nice home, and a successful life. We attended church regularly and found a small group of other couples to hang out with in our free time. We were polite, educated, and generally considered to be happy and well-adjusted. We even believed it to be true.

Our first child, Jessica, was born in February 1994, two weeks before I graduated from Palmer College of Chiropractic. Suddenly our married life flipped from being about us to being about her. I have never been as excited as I was to see my precious little girl come into this life, and to this day I can recall the exact size and look of her newborn form. Starting a new practice in Illinois, raising a baby girl, and leaving the pressures and frustrations of college behind us, we were ready to kick-start our lives, to make our family into something beautiful, and to enjoy the benefits of the sacrifices we both had made.

I remember Paige beaming with pride and joy when she showed everyone our daughter. She was so happy, so excited, and maybe even a bit scared at the same time. So was I. We rented our first real home—a two-bedroom apartment—and got our first taste of family living.

Paige became a stay-at-home mom, and I began building my new practice. I was Dr. Brad Mathias now. For fifty to sixty hours a week, I kept my nose to the grindstone, working for my soon-to-be retired father, Dr. Gerald Mathias. He was eager to give me the reins and trade this prairie town for the Blue Ridge Mountains of Virginia. Soon every hour of every day was full to the brim. I joined Rotary, we attended the local Methodist church, and Paige was involved with MOPS (Mothers of Preschoolers). We were settling in, growing roots and predictability.

By 1998, I was a workaholic with a thriving, successful practice. Our family had grown too. Bethany Rose, our second daughter, was born in 1995, and our son, Caleb, arrived in 1997. Paige was as stressed and overwhelmed as any mother of three kids under the age of four—compounded by living with an absentee husband who seemed to have time for everyone but her.

Paige began to grow some significant anger, and I continued to "adapt." I endured her resentment over my work, pointing out that as a professional it was my obligation to care for my patients and work late hours, answer after-hours calls, and play golf with the local leaders. It was my duty to meet our family's needs, and I was providing for her every "want" along the way.

She had a new house on the golf course, a brand new minivan, a white picket fence (literally) in the backyard, and a time-share in Florida. We wanted for nothing on the outside, but on the inside we were struggling to sustain any kind of personal affection or connection. Paige was a reserved, shy, brand-new member of my hometown community and had to work harder than I did at making new friends; I was extroverted and had trouble saying no to anyone. Our growing personality conflicts, normal for couples in their fifth or sixth year of marriage, were amplified by three small children, isolation, and fatigue—all overshadowed by my narcissism.

It didn't take long for the wheels of our marriage to come off completely. What had once seemed to be a promising future and a perfect family dissolved into a shell of its former self. I was beginning to develop some serious anger toward my wife. I was working hard to support my growing family, run my practice, and stay involved in the community—all while dealing with what seemed from my self-centered perspective to be an ungrateful and nagging wife.

In my frustration and anger, I reached out to a close friend for consolation. That relationship eventually led to an affair. I was still "adapting" to the situation, seeking to maintain the outward facade of a healthy and balanced life. But on the inside I was alone, afraid, and weary of trying to make everyone in my life happy.

I hid the affair from everyone but a dear friend. I shared it with him after getting drunk one night at his business office after a Rotary dinner. I barely remembered telling him, but he didn't forget. It was this friend who, over a year later, told another mutual friend about my infidelity. That man then told his wife, who told my wife. The situation culminated in Paige's phone call in the middle of the night, venting her pent-up rage, anger, and frustration at me as I lay in a beater hotel room in Lake Geneva, Wisconsin.

After seven years of adapting, accommodating, and trying to make my wife and everyone I knew happy, I had successfully created a false self. I had disassociated my actions from reality and justified all I was and did by the approval of those around me. I was false from the inside out—fake, foolish, and now exposed. My marriage was officially ending, and I had no one to blame but myself.

Over and Done

The problem was that, by then, I didn't care about our marriage. I didn't care about Paige, myself, or anyone else. I didn't want to be married to anyone; I didn't want to rely on any other person ever again! I had walked away from the affair and still found my life miserable. After a decade of sacrifice and extraordinarily hard work, I had lost all my savings and financial successes, I had lost my professional reputation, and I had lost my honor and my credibility as a man, as a husband, as a *father*. I was dead on the inside.

Despite my failures, I believed I just needed a new start. I knew I didn't love my wife like a husband should, and I couldn't keep "adapting" to try to feel in love with her, or to help her feel in love with me. I could tell that Paige didn't really want to be married to me anymore either. She wanted a man to love her and help her raise our three kids as a true husband should. She wanted a man who was stable, predictable, and consistent—three things I wasn't ever going to be.

Even before Paige learned about the affair, I had tried to leave our marriage "gracefully." I had suggested that she would be better off without me, that I no longer had feelings for her. Our physical intimacy had been gone for years, and I hadn't felt connected to her since our third child had been born in 1997.

Paige's response was to ask for counseling. She said we needed to get help from a professional, attend church more regularly, and work on repairing our relationship. I didn't want help, hated church, and was about to be done with playing any more relationship games. After my affair, I thought I knew what genuine passion and acceptance and happiness felt like—and our marriage was missing them all.

Several months before Paige found out about my affair, I had a job offer in Wisconsin. I took it, knowing that Paige would not move again. We stayed married, but only by the thinnest of legal technicalities. She didn't file for divorce, and I didn't ask for one. I sent checks home twice a month and visited the kids and her every weekend. But for all practical purposes, I was gone.

When she received the call from her best friend back in Illinois with news of my adultery, it was the anvil that broke the camel's back. Paige was mortified to learn of my infidelity. Despite our troubles, despite our lack of intimacy and my physical absence, she had clung to the idea of keeping our marriage alive. That hope ended with her late-night phone call.

All her rage, all her frustration and feelings of betrayal spewed out of her that night. As I sat in the hotel room, I could almost physically feel her words sting my ears as I listened to her vent seven years of heartache and pain. I could tell by her tone and her never-before-spoken profanities aimed squarely at me that this family was about to officially end.

Divorce and Delay

I received the certified letter at my office in Lake Geneva a few days later, solemnly served to me by a local county sheriff's deputy. It was as expected: Paige had gone through with her threats. I held the divorce paperwork, brimming with complex language and descriptions of required responses, hearings, affidavits, and pending legal depositions. It was inches thick and sounded as angry as official words can.

I sighed, put the paperwork in a drawer, and refocused on work. I had already put my failed marriage behind me. I was deeply regretful of the pain I had caused Paige as a husband and friend, but I had decided just to move on and start over as soon as I could, for her sake and mine. She really wanted a husband who would be there for her every hour of every day, and I was *not* that guy. But I was confident that she would find someone very quickly. As long I could be with my three children every other weekend and holiday, I was more than willing to let her go.

Nine months later, I was well down the road to a new life, but my wife seemed fixated on the past. My contact with Paige was limited, as I lived in another state and only saw her for a few moments twice a month when we switched off with the kids on the weekends. But whenever we met, I could tell she absolutely hated me. I was tolerant of her anger, knowing I had failed her and betrayed her, but it seemed to me she wasn't even trying to move forward. She was frustrated, angry, and resentful almost every time I saw her—while I was upbeat, relaxed, and refocused on life.

After all, for the first time ever, I wasn't "adapting"; I wasn't being forced to pretend or fake my way through a day. I could just be me, and I was reveling in the freedom of that reality. I was deeply buried in my work, had a few new friendships, and had even started to date again, believing my old life was over and a new one had begun. I had walked away from any form of Christian faith and was openly study-ing different religions to see what might make the most sense to me.

I had instructed my attorney to give Paige whatever she wanted in the divorce. I had made no legal moves to restrict her financially or put any pressure on her for custody or assets. I truly had no agenda except to get on with my life. I just wanted to see my kids every other weekend and holiday. That seemed the best solution for everyone, and I was puzzled by the delay in those conditions being accepted by Paige and her attorney.

After eleven months of waiting, I still had not received the final divorce paperwork. I had almost forgotten I wasn't technically di-vorced. Paige had relocated to Memphis to be with her family; I was fully distracted by my new career and relationships in Wisconsin. I spoke of her as being my "ex" and believed it to be true, expecting a final signed document in my mailbox any day—formally declaring the end of our marital state.

It never came.

Divine Intervention

Over a year after my wife and I split, I had a vision. A serious and un-explainable supernatural experience. It happened while I was sick—as sick as I have ever been. I was lying in bed, suffering from a severe middle-ear infection. A fever and abscess had formed near my central nervous system, and the doctors had done surgery to ease the pres-sure. If the antibiotics kicked in, all would be fine. If they didn't, I risked life-threatening complications.

Lying there, exhausted and alone, I reflected on my thirty-two years of living and felt a bit ashamed of my life, the choices I had made, how I had acted, and how my kids would never really know their dad. I decided if there was a possibility that I might not pull out of this, I needed to get some stuff sorted out. So I uttered a simple prayer. I only wanted to know if there was a God and if he, she, or it cared at all about me.

I was sincere in my simple request. I had studied both ancient and modern religious teachings of many faiths and customs; I had researched Eastern mysticism, Mormonism, Satanism, Universalism, Lutheranism, Scientology, Islam, Hinduism, and finally Wicca. All told, I had read dozens of books and reviews of various faiths and had concluded that there was probably no single God, but rather a sacred truth in the vitality of the earth as a holy object that deserved our love and admiration and respect. I became a tree hugger.

As I lay in bed, I suddenly felt and saw things that were not in the room. I had a profound sense of something or someone much greater, much larger than any person could be. I somehow experienced God in person that day—Jesus, in fact. I was shown my life in two states: as it would be unaltered and as it could become if I chose to surrender to this truth.

It's hard to describe in words, but suffice it to say that I was radically affected by this encounter. My fever and my infection vanished; in just a moment, my mind and body became clear and healthy.

I could tell you only a few things for sure at that instant: I was no longer sick; I had just experienced Jesus for myself; and this Christianity stuff was for real. Then I began to feel a deep and profound sense of loss at the failure of my marriage and at the compromise of the covenant I had made with God and with Paige. So strong was this sense of injustice and angst that I got up, dressed, and immediately drove to Memphis.

Twelve hours later I showed up at the door of my kids' new home. Their mother was waiting for me. I had called to tell them I was coming, and an amazed Paige had asked why. Living three states and a thousand miles away, one didn't just hop in the car and commute to see the kids. I didn't know how to explain it. I tried, but I kept choking up. The tears kept drowning my words as I attempted to describe what had just happened to me, but she got the gist of it and allowed me to come without a full explanation.

Inside, I was exploding. It felt like something very important had just clicked into place for me, as if a huge puzzle piece that had been missing was suddenly found. Life was beginning to return to my heart and my soul. I never cried—maybe twice in thirty-two years—but on that twelve-hour pilgrimage to Memphis, I wept like a baby. I cried for my past sins and failures. I cried for my kids, for my lost marriage, and for the ridiculously selfish things I had done. I cried for joy and for happiness at finally finding something, someone to believe in.

I wept as I felt the heart of God breaking for my family and me. I shuddered as I thought of all the pain and tragedy I had created along the way. I wasn't returning to Memphis to save my marriage or prevent a divorce—I was going to be reconciled and to start my new life in Christ. No more holding back, no more pretending. I was totally ready to repent, to relocate, to reconnect however God wanted me to. I was done making decisions on my own, and I was done trying to figure things out.

On that drive I had no idea that God might actually be planning a resurrection—to raise the burnt ashes of my marriage from the dead, as he had raised his son, Jesus, from the literal grave.

But he did just that.

A year later, Paige and I were fully reconciled, living together with our three children in Germantown, Tennessee. It was a miracle. We were a family again, rebuilding a life and a home that had been in ruins only months before. God, in his power and purpose, had shown my wife that I had indeed been changed. He encouraged her to trust him with our marriage restoration, as much as she had trusted him in my absence.

Just a few weeks before I had my incredible experience with Jesus, Paige had uttered a powerful prayer in which she surrendered me, the kids, and her stability to God. She was genuinely ready to let go and move on. She stopped praying primarily for the restitution of our marriage and instead began praying for me, that I would let Jesus take control of my life. She prayed Scripture for me as well, including Ephesians 1:17: "I keep asking that the God of our Lord Jesus Christ, the glorious Father, may give you the Spirit of wisdom and revelation, so that you may know him better" (NIV).

In those moments of release, I believe God acted, and by the power of his Holy Spirit he began to move in both of us to accept the impossible, to begin a process of full and complete restoration back into the marriage covenant of our youth. For the first time, I was able to be truly honest with Paige, sharing all my thoughts, fears, and beliefs. She in turn seemed to be much stronger and more focused in her faith, unfazed by my issues or the baggage of the past.

It took several long counseling sessions, active accountability, and long-term rebuilding of my integrity with my in-laws, friends, and family. But in the end God was able to demonstrate his divine power in our lives by restoring our marriage and preventing us from becoming just another statistic.

The Road to Recovery

Our journey back into recovery, although miraculous, was not easy. I don't want to gloss over the many issues of trust, consistency, and integrity that needed to be overcome in the following years, but it's accurate to say that God did indeed rapidly restore our marriage and our home.

What is most difficult to portray is the lasting impact of my infidelity and the brokenness of our marriage on our three precious children. When our family came back together, Jessica was eight, Bethany was seven, and Caleb was five. The turmoil created from the verbal grenades Paige and I had hurled back and forth for months, followed by my absence, imprinted numerous profound memories on their young lives, and the impact of those emotional traumas was unavoidable.

Jessica was especially aware that something bad had occurred, and she knew that it had to do with Daddy leaving Mommy for someone else. Jessica sensed that she had to be a helper to her mom, because she was the oldest and Dad wasn't around, so she immediately matured before her time.

Bethany developed a deep sense of almost constant anxiety about being left by me or Paige. She was fearful that if she went to sleep at night she might die and not wake up at all—or awake all alone with no one to care for her.

Caleb was very young during the earliest of our fights and remained very quiet, sullen, and angry at me for most of the first year I was back. He was jealous of his mom and didn't even seem to know why. He kept his distance from me emotionally and physically and got very irritable whenever Paige was gone and I had to care for him alone. It was obvious that at first he resented my being around at all, as if it were an intrusion into his normal world.

For all three of my children, I believe these struggles were directly attributable to the fifteen months of separation and instability that took its toll on our home.

Over the next seven years, God orchestrated a series of events in my work, Paige's work, and our Christian faith to direct us out of the Memphis area into Nashville. From my professional work as a chiropractic physician, I moved into the executive management of Christian ministry and media. During those changes, our relocation, and the shifts in our schedules, there was always a sense of unease connected to Bethany's fears and Jessica's need for control. Caleb was the most laid-back about it all, slowly warming to having a life in which being with his dad was more normal again.

Given the very public nature of my failings as a husband, I never tried to hide the events of my past from my three kids. I was very open with them about the general details of our marital separation, openly admitted my role in the "almost divorce," and asked for their forgiveness. I did all of that, in tears on my knees, with them and their mother in the living room of their Germantown home the day after my experience with Jesus.

Over time as my kids grew older and more mature, I was able to fill in some of the details of our past marital problems, with edited specifics about my affair and lack of integrity. They seemed to be able to process the past, while reconciling it with the current reality of Paige and I being back together and living in harmony. On occasion the kids would overhear a heated argument between their mom and me and would creep closer to our bedroom door to listen and see if everything was okay. No matter how far we had come in restoring balance and peace in our home, the past still loomed over us, reminding us that our family's new happiness could come crashing down at any moment.

It took at least five years of my careful and consistent behavior as a father and husband before my kids began to relax, to trust that our home was really back to the way it was supposed to be. Gradually they felt more confident that Dad wasn't leaving, that Mom wouldn't throw Dad out in the heat of a disagreement, and that their parents were resolved, determined, and working to make their marriage better.

As Paige and I grew stronger and our family became more cohesive, many of the kids' fears and concerns slowly subsided. Caleb, who used to sneak into our room almost every night to sleep with us, started to stay in his own bed. Jessica, who had seemed determined to help make every parenting decision for her sister and brother, began to trust that Mom and Dad might know what we were doing as parents and that she could just be the older sister. Bethany, however, continued to struggle with her fears and anxieties, often needing Paige to repeat at her bedside "You're not going to die" two or three times in a row before she could fall asleep.

It's impossible to say how much my failings as a father and husband injured the mental and emotional health of my kids and my wife. But it was painfully clear to me that the years of our strained and dysfunctional "almost divorce" had left some long-term scars. I can't imagine the hurt and turbulence in families who live with the reality of divorce and shared custody every day for years on end.

As Paige and I were growing in our mutual trust, love, and respect, our marriage was becoming publicly restored and strengthened, leading to our increased involvement at church and in couples' ministry. We found that many couples had endured infidelity, and worse. A lot of families in the local church were struggling with similar if not identical issues in their own homes. They needed to see an example, a real-life testimony to the ability of God to fix the seemingly unfixable. They needed to find hope and encouragement in our story and see that the God who had saved our family could save theirs, too. Suddenly our painful past took on significance and purpose. From our loss and regrets emerged new hope, grace, and confidence for others to take the same journey we had taken.

It amazed me to see how powerfully God had recovered what I had lost, how his redemptive work not only recovered our marriage but made it stronger and more beautiful—a testament to his power to resurrect even things that were completely dead. Since the day I drove to Memphis to ask for forgiveness, my love for my wife and the pattern of our lives have shifted dramatically. We have changed in ways I never could have imagined. It's the same with everyone who discovers the power of grace and love in Jesus.

But even with the miraculous work God had done in our lives, my fears for my kids began to grow when puberty and adolescence hit. Hormones, crushes, pop culture, body image, and public school all became huge issues at one time or another with each of our kids. Every time there was a crisis brewing, I found myself wondering if their problems were a delayed time bomb of my own making, ticking from a fuse that I had unintentionally lit years earlier.

It's not a good way to live, but the fear and the guilt were always there—just under the surface of my mind, waiting to pounce on me and prove to everyone how screwed up I really was. How much I had lost and failed. How responsible I still felt for all the problems my family had to endure. It was crippling, and it often kept me from taking parenting action to correct my kids when they needed it. I frequently held back, worried that they would resent me or disrespect my authority.

This led me to parent mostly out of fear and not love, a theme that will be explored further in other parts of our story. Suffice it to say, this fear-and-guilt cycle sometimes paralyzed me and other times tempted me to overreact to the failings of my kids as I began to see ghosts of my own past haunt their lives. Although anyone from the outside could have seen that these issues were mostly normal behaviors common to any family with tweens and teens, I was convinced at times that they were in fact punishment for my compromised living a decade before. I had great anxiety about how I could ever hope to lead my kids into the future as a father without creating further problems for their lives and my own. It would take a family crisis years later to shake me out of this personal pattern once and for all.

*   *   *

Our prologue is a significant part of our family's complicated history and provides context for our road trip adventures eight years later. Your own family's history may not include the same dramatic failures and victories, but every family has baggage: issues from the past that threaten to derail the future. I'm willing to bet that most parents sometimes look at their kids' problems and feel shame and guilt, wondering if their past parenting decisions or poor choices contributed to their children's struggles. If you're in that place and are parenting out of fear, have courage—and read on.

FLASHBACK AT THE FALLS

Trust in the LORD with all your heart, and do not lean on your own understanding. In all your ways acknowledge him, and he will make straight your paths. PROVERBS 3:5-6, ESV

June 2010

Hiking along the sapphire blue shores of one of the most beautiful lakes in the world, I found myself invigorated and out of breath. The combination of high altitude, frigid morning air, and the thirty-pound backpack I was carrying caused me to pause on the trail. Looking back over my shoulder, I saw my little band of intrepid flatlander suburbanites following dutifully behind me as we crossed this magnificent mountain landscape. We were exploring a remote seven-mile trail to Bow Falls that skirts the picturesque Bow Lake in Alberta, Canada, located only a few miles from the idyllic Lake Louise resort region of Banff. We had left our rental cabin before dawn that day, hoping to get on the trail in time to reach our isolated destination by noon.

I had led my family from Nashville, Tennessee, to Canada on a quest to reintroduce them to the Author of all beauty, the Creator of true life, Jesus Christ. I could envision no place in the world that could convey the majesty and creativity of their spiritual heritage better than this remarkable piece of paradise.

An avid hiker and road warrior, I had visited Alberta several times before with my lifelong friend Brian Hardin. As a professional photographer, he had explored this lake with me, and I had kept one of his pictures framed in my living room ever since. Bow Lake was a sacred place for me. I had wept on the day I first stood on its shores. Dramatic mountain walls swept down into a crystal-clear, glacier-fed lake that perfectly reflected the snowcapped peaks from every angle. This valley had been designated a UNESCO World Heritage site. Every summer, tourist buses swept by its shores following the world-famous Icefields Parkway—an ice-trail road running from Banff to Jasper—carrying hundreds of visitors eager to see the sights, buy the trinkets, and pose for pictures. These drive-by gazers were content to leave the majesty of the lake's shores with a few digital memories. In their rush to see more, did they truly understand or appreciate the silent and awesome presence of this pristine wilderness? I doubted it.

When I stand on the shores of this lake, I always feel as if I am standing in the presence of my Creator God. No other place in the world moves me like this place does. It is unique, special, unequaled in its beauty and its serenity. So when I had an opportunity to take a trip with my family, it didn't take me long to decide where we would go. Now here we were, hiking past the well-worn shoreline of the casual tourist trail and heading to the soaring glacier's edge, which in summer forms the magnificent Bow Falls, rising over five hundred feet in the far distance.

The trail was long and winding, with very few easy stretches, and we quickly realized it would tax us much more than any trail we had tried before. My sophisticated teens were excited, engaged, and anxiously snapping pictures as they hiked. Exclaiming like little children who had just discovered another new ride at Disneyland, they shared their joy with anyone who would listen. I smiled at their random outbursts of oohs and aahs, their pointing and yelling at the wildlife and mountain scenery around us:

"Dad, this is AMAZING! It's soooooo cool."

"Are those elk? Are they dangerous?"

"Is that an eagle? How cool is that!"

"Seriously, are there bears up here? Will they eat us?"

They would each exclaim their discoveries or shout their delight, as if they alone had seen the beauty and we risked missing a critical life moment if we didn't immediately stop and stare with them before it suddenly disappeared. It was awesome to see my suburban, media-addicted teenagers running around the wilderness like kids in a candy store. It was a prayer answered—and a major passion of my life shared with my family for the first time.

I sensed something critical happening in them at this remote, wild, and beautiful mountain. God was present for them like he had been for me. They were seeing the majesty of the mystical and mysterious Creator we worshiped together every Sunday. Only this time, they were worshiping spontaneously, without me leading or prompting them.

As I paused by the trail, my mind flashed back to that devastating night my family had experienced not even a year ago. The events that had shaped our decision to be here were painful memories, yet the sting of them was already fading in the magic of this moment. Nevertheless, that shockingly unexpected crisis had formed in my wife and me the resolution to change our lives, to adapt our parenting in ways I never would have dreamed of a few months earlier. That priority shift resulted in our decision to drive our entire family seven thousand miles in two weeks in an effort to reconnect with each other, and in the process, we saw our journey connect us all with God. Here is our story. . . .

September 2009

I could tell something was wrong. Even in the midst of my hectic schedule and the busyness of everyday life, I had noticed changes in my middle child, a shift in her mood and appearance over the past few months. She had withdrawn a bit—removed herself from our simple weekly family life, sat out our evening dinner discussions, and always had too much to do on family movie nights. She was still there, physically present, but she was emotionally "checked out."

Bethany had begun to fade into a shell of her normally dramatic and exuberant teenage self. She was still an athletic, slim, blonde "Barbie doll" of a girl, but her beautiful sky-blue eyes had seemed to lose their color. They were darker now, especially with the extra mascara and eyeliner she had begun to wear. Her skin looked more frail and white than I'd ever remembered. She kept her eyes down, usually with a hoodie over her head and iPod earbuds jammed in her ears. She was trying to keep us all out. It was frustrating, irritating, and disrespectful, and I had made a mental note to confront her about the many rude behaviors I had observed in her recently.

My patience for her teenage angst had worn thin. She needed to be corrected. It was time our family quit being punished by her unpredictable moods and her annoyance with everyone and everything around her.

I loved her dearly, but I had to admit it—Bethany could be a real snot sometimes. Her older sister and younger brother were always complaining about her attitudes and selfishness, and on more than one occasion Paige had thrown up her hands in frustration and despair, wondering if Bethany would *ever* grow up. It didn't take a PhD to figure out that we were giving her way too much latitude. Her schoolwork was starting to suffer, and seemingly overnight she had changed her clothes from a well-groomed "preppy" style to a sloppy, skinny jeans "skater" look. What was going on with her?

Whatever it was, I assumed it was related to her growing hormonal imbalances, combined with girl-boy teen drama and high school social stress. I also assumed her attitude was a jab at her mother and me, an attempt to show us that she was older and independent now, able to handle herself without our help. So I, the supposedly wise father, was already judging her actions as rebellious and in need of correction before I had talked with her at all. I was seriously right—and I was seriously wrong.

In retrospect, the signs were there, if I had taken the time to notice. If I had been paying attention to Bethany, really paying attention, I would have seen the faint scars from a few old, purple cuts—long, swollen, twisted welts—as well as the chronic scars on the insides of her forearms. But I didn't. I might have noticed that the girl who had once been the most voracious eater in the family was suffering from an ongoing loss of appetite. I might have noticed that her choice of music, art, and reading had shifted from bright and uplifting to dark and depressing. She had, in fact, been morphing from an animated and optimistic young woman, full of life, hope, and excitement, into a shadow of her healthier self.

In my naiveté, I was still remembering her as she was before, instead of seeing her as she had become. I had missed the transformation in front of my very eyes. Actually, I'd seen the symptoms, but I hadn't taken them seriously. Instead of investigating the sudden changes in my daughter, I'd dismissed them, chalking it all up to normal teen issues. Day after hectic day had come and gone, and I was blindly doing my best to keep everything and everyone in their proper places. Hypnotized by the repetitive schedules and demands on my time, I was slowly losing my awareness of the very real and dangerous problem growing in my own home. I had fallen asleep at the wheel.

Not only had Bethany changed in appearance and attitude, but the time she spent alone in her room and away from her family or friends had grown from a few hours each week to a few hours each day. When she was around, her blank and absent stare was devoid of any emotion—beyond her growing irritation with the rest of us. Yet I continued to misread her activities, changes in appearance, and nasty attitude. I shudder to think what might have happened that dark week in September 2009 if I hadn't taken a moment to pray with my wife late one night in our bedroom.

Divine Intervention

As I took the time to quiet myself, and as I emptied my mind of the day's worries, I opened my heart in prayer and immediately felt the presence of God intrude into my awareness. It was like a firm, tender, but powerful impression, a deep whisper in my mind: *Ask Bethany what she is hiding from you.* I thought, *Tonight, Lord? Right now?* My heart felt an intense surge of emotion as I sensed the urgency. *Immediately!*

Since committing my life radically to Christ eight years earlier, one thing I had learned is that when God clearly speaks to me, it's wise to respond right away. My wife and I agreed it was important enough to interrupt our sleep that night, and we decided to find out what was really going on with our daughter.

As we walked the short distance from our room to hers, I felt frustration and anger build within me. Obviously Bethany was lying to us about something, and I was determined to find out what. Like many parents, we had battled with the pattern of deceit and half-truths so common in adolescents. I was convinced that Bethany had lied to us once again and was secretly pursuing some defiant violation of our house rules regarding boys or Facebook or texting. She was always pushing the boundaries with us, and this time she must have gone too far. After all, the middle child is often the most difficult—everyone told us so. Bethany had fought her mother and me every step of the way, ever since she was a little toddler. "I DO IT!" she had screamed at us when she first learned to talk and walk. And in the next decade, it seemed she had continued to resist every effort we made as her parents to win her heart and her trust.

Reality Check

At the door to my daughter's bedroom, I paused and listened. I could hear her quiet sobs and restless movements. I was beginning to grow more concerned and less angry at whatever she had done. I began to feel a darkness—deep pain and despair—coming from her room. It was a palpable sense that something or someone was tormenting my daughter.

I had often felt unprepared and unqualified to raise a daughter, let alone two. I seemed unable to understand their unique emotional needs. Yet I knew for sure that I loved Bethany with all my heart, and I was ready to do anything for her. Like any father, I would take a bullet to the brain or a knife through my heart—whatever it took to protect her. But that night, I sensed something deeper and more terrifying trying to harm my child, something I couldn't touch, fight, or repulse.

Whatever this problem was, it threatened to destroy my daughter, and it was time for me to battle for her like I had never done before. I immediately began to pray and to seek the wisdom of my Lord and Savior Jesus Christ. Rarely do we get to pray for something else as pure and as needed as wisdom in raising our children, and I was exceedingly short and to the point. *Lord, I need some insight here for Bethany. Please, Lord. I'm scared and confused, and I don't know how to help her. Please, God.* And again I sensed the peaceful but firm impression in my mind: *Just ask her to reveal what she has hidden.*

Bethany by now was restlessly moving in her bed; maybe she could sense that someone was at her door. As her mother and I entered and approached her bedside, she moved suddenly as if to hide something. When we turned on the hall light and its illumination flooded her dark room, we could tell by Bethany's swollen eyes that she had been crying for some time. Embarrassed, she quickly got up and turned her face, trying to wipe away the evidence of her weakness.

My wife and I simply told our daughter that we felt God had revealed to us in prayer that she had been struggling with a profound and painful secret. We assured her that we wanted to help, but to do that we would need her to be completely honest about whatever was going on in her life. As we gently but firmly asked her to reveal what she was hiding from us, it seemed her entire body shuddered with the impact of our words. Instead of denying her actions, she slowly sat down and began to weep into her hands. This was *not* the reaction she usually had when we confronted her about inappropriate behavior. This was the response of a broken and devastated soul, weary and hopeless and alone.

I remember the sudden and painful tightening in my gut, the nausea in the back of my throat as I listened to my little girl tell me she had been molested—touched inappropriately by a male student in her middle school, the day of her graduation from eighth grade. *How that could be? Why didn't she tell us?* Dozens of thoughts and questions invaded my mind like a tidal wave. I watched helplessly while my wife erupted into tears and smothered my daughter's little frame with her protective hug.

The nausea inside me quickly grew into numbness. My mind refused to accept what my ears had just heard, and I almost shut down with the emotional shock of her revelation. *Not my family! Not my daughter, not in my house!* As my fear and shock subsided, my rage surged—rage at whoever had done this, rage at my inability to fix this terrible wound in my Bethany, rage at my own failure to protect her from harm, from violation. I choked as I tried to absorb it all. Why had this happened? What was going on in my own family? And why didn't I have a clue?

Something much worse and much different from a secret boyfriend or an abuse of freedom had occurred. In my haste to confront and correct, I had missed the other possible explanation for my daughter's progressive changes in attitude, appearance, and behavior: despair.

The space between defiance and despair is very small. As a parent, I had yet to learn the difference, and given the history of Bethany's stubborn and persistent personality, I had categorized her in my mind as a "strong-willed child." Long before this terrible night I had judged her incapable of being forthright, truthful, or respectful, and so at the apex of her young life, I had rushed to a premature judgment of my daughter's motives long before the facts were revealed. In that moment I had a parental epiphany: Bethany wasn't acting so strange because of some stereotypical teenage funk; she was acting out of pain. Her world had grown increasingly dark as her heart gave way to despair and shame. She had carefully hidden her pain from us, fearing we would not understand or continue to love her like before.

As a father, that moment broke my heart. I realized in an instant how foolish I had been, how easily I had assumed the worst of my daughter, and how legalistically my own religious nature had intruded upon the most fragile of life moments. If I had continued in the path of correction and confrontation that night with my daughter, I believe I might have lost her forever. Instead, by the amazing grace of God alone, I kept myself from launching into another angry tirade at her deception and intuitively was able to grasp that her actions were being caused *by* her secret, not in an effort to protect it.

Bethany sobbed and rocked back and forth in her chair as she told her mother and me in a rush of words and gasping cries of her attempt to take her own life a day before. She told us how she had been cutting herself, desperate to stop the pain and shame of being molested four months earlier. She begged us to believe her and forgive her and protect her and help her. Her words were like broken glass as they hit my heart, ripping away at my hardened beliefs and deepest fears.

A long night ensued, filled with explanations, choking cries of despair and shame, and anger at God for letting this happen and at myself for leaving her all alone to figure it out. Anger for the many nights she had cried herself to sleep, only to wake up to the same sense of unrelenting fear and guilt. For victims of molestation and abuse, the irrational feelings of guilt and condemnation are overwhelmingly intense. The fear that somehow they had caused the incident, the anger at being helpless to prevent it, and the deep identity-shattering belief that they deserved it—all this forms an inner core of despair so devastating it often leads them to contemplate taking their own lives, just to end the pain. My daughter, my precious and beautiful child, had been mistreated, abused, and then isolated by her fears and my prejudices to a point where she felt her best option was to take her own life rather than confide in us, the ones whose greatest role was to protect, nurture, and love her into adulthood.

My shame was well-deserved; hers was not. To say that I felt remorse, regret, and guilt at my failure to recognize her condition is a monumental understatement. My heart burned with the pain not only of my daughter but also of my heavenly Father as I realized how little I really knew my own child. How little of a genuine relationship I shared with her. How much I had wrongly assumed about her. The lies I had agreed to believe about her life and her attitudes. I had somehow lost touch with my daughter to such a degree that she couldn't take her greatest crisis to me for help and counsel and comfort. In effect, when she needed me the most, I was no longer there. Paige, too, was heartsick at hearing Bethany describe what had happened. As her mother, Paige had always been there to protect her children and felt grieved to the core that this time, she hadn't. She wanted to reverse time, to go back and protect her daughter from all this suffering.

Such was the shock and surprise at the night's events that I had to step back and consciously calm myself in a moment of prayer and sacred Scripture reading. Accepting my failures, I was determined to learn, grow, and improve in my God-given role as Bethany's earthly father. I began the process of rearranging my schedule, my priorities, and my life to a substantial degree and began asking God to show me what I could do to help repair the wounds in my daughter and in our home. Over time, that prayer for healing, wholeness, and restoration would be answered in a most unusual way.

STEPPING BACK FROM THE EDGE OF FEAR

Face your fears head-on. Drop the fig leaf; come out from hiding. For how long? Longer than you want to; long enough to raise the deeper issues, let the wound surface from beneath it all. Losing the false self is painful; though it's a mask, it's one we've worn for years and losing it can feel like losing a close friend. Underneath the mask is all the hurt and fear we've been running from, hiding from. To let it come to the surface can shake us like an earthquake. JOHN ELDREDGE, *WILD AT HEART*

TO GET FROM WHERE we were in chapter 1 all the way to Bow Lake almost a year later, Paige and I struggled through a very difficult time as parents and spouses. Living with the fallout of a crisis like ours is not a simple process. Like the trail to Bow Falls, our path to recovery had many twists and turns. Some portions of our trek were full of rocks and uneven ground. Others were beautiful vistas of discovery and illumination. But every step was an adventure. Along the way we discovered many truths we needed to grasp about God and about our lives as parents.

Reset

It took several weeks to begin processing what we had discovered about our Bethany. I had been badly shaken by how little I really knew my daughter—and how overconfident I had been in my own abilities to parent, provide, and protect. The emotional and mental shock from learning about my daughter's molestation and near suicide had sent me into a hyperdrive of fear, anxiety, guilt, and self-directed anger, alternating in erratic cycles and leaving me profoundly uneasy and restless.

When I allowed myself to review the sequence of events in my daughter's past, I could see there had been many of the issues, challenges, and at times overtly rebellious behavior so common to teens. But I had failed to recognize the true nature of her actions, and in missing that, I had failed to prevent something terrible from happening. I wanted—no, needed—to understand how it had come to that point. I wanted to reach some sort of conclusion, to replay each event in the weeks before her crisis from a variety of perspectives, all spinning over and over in my mind. I was desperate to find out what I could have done differently to avoid the whole tragic situation.

My mind pinwheeled with the same questions: For how long had she considered suicide as an option? Were there hints or suggestions that I had ignored? What could I have done better as her dad? I should have noticed her pain and her despair much sooner. Could I have

acted more decisively? I should have pushed her for the reason behind her bad moods. Where had the time gone from her just being
a little girl to becoming this tortured teen? I was constantly haunted
by these unanswerable questions, revisiting all my mistakes and failed
observations a thousand times and in a thousand different ways. It was
devastating for me to admit how badly I had miscalculated the state of
my own family and in particular the fragile condition of my daughter.

I'm a great guilt-trip guy. I was taught by my parents and from my
earliest church days that a good Christian was a "guilty" one. Being
free of guilt meant that you didn't understand how holy God was
and how messed up you really were. I had absorbed the hellfire-and-
brimstone tagline to the bone. So when a tragic event occurred in my
life, I already knew deep down it was all because of me. Add to that
my own past and profound failings at being a faithful husband and
a present father, and I was wrapped up in a chain of guilt so heavy I
was emotionally and spiritually paralyzed.

Fear and Anger

I felt like I had completely failed Bethany as a father. In my ignorance, blinded by my own presumption and apathy, I had almost
allowed my family to slide over the edge of a fatal cliff. By the time
we found out about Bethany's crisis, we were only inches away from
plunging into a chasm of irreversible loss and tragedy. It was a sobering moment for us all, and it led to six months of life-changing
introspection about what I thought I already knew about parenting,
our family, and my faith.

I knew that we had survived by God's grace alone. By his faithfulness, we were allowed a second chance to stop our family from
experiencing the most devastating loss a parent can endure, and we
found ourselves worn and weary in the aftermath of it all.

I felt as if I no longer deserved to be the leader of my home. As Bethany's father, I knew I should have been the one to step up and carry the responsibility of my daughter's safety and well-being. I immediately began looking for ways to pay my penance for all my failures as her dad. But in my guilt and pain, I realized that the only way to restore the loss of my daughter's innocence and happiness would be to reverse time—literally change the revolutions of the planet we lived on and go back to a simpler period. Maybe to when she was five and full of blonde curls, giggles, and simple innocence. Then I would start fresh with her and keep her safe by never ever letting her out of my sight again. Either that or I could lock her up in our basement for the rest of her life. I wanted so badly to reset from the situation we were stuck in, and I wanted to have my little girl back just the way she had been.

As active as we were in church, I was uncomfortable reaching out to anyone there. Instead, I began searching my faith for some answers, some guidance. Maybe if I took extra time each day with my Bible, I could discern a new spiritual truth that would help to fix Bethany. If I could just integrate all the best teaching books I could find on parenting and insert some new biblical insight, maybe I could discover a brand-new parenting "formula" to help me raise my kids safely from here on.

I wanted to find a guarantee for parenting that would keep my kids from ever experiencing such pain again. If my wife and I could ensure that no further harm would ever come to our daughter, then we could start to relax, maybe even enjoy life again. Yet as I read, prayed, and logically reviewed my options, I realized that to do that, we would have to create the ultimate parenting cocoon, so strong and so complete that no one could ever break its protective barrier. That was impossible, which meant that the problem of protection would not go away; the fear remained. And even if we could some-how magically alter our life circumstances, it might help us take care of the threats from outside, but what could we do about the stuff that was already let in?

It didn't take long for me to realize that with all my repeated day-dreams of impossible scenarios, I was still only reacting. As a typical dad, I was wired to solve problems, not understand what created them. I was not keen on serious introspection, on taking the time to consider what would really help Bethany to heal and cope with her pain. I was much more concerned about me as her father doing my job better, to prove to her and to myself that I could still be an effective dad.

Eventually I had to face the truth: I lacked the ability either to change the past or to prevent Bethany from future harm. Just as I'd had to admit how wrong I'd been about so much with my daughter, I now had to admit I was equally inadequate at solving her problems in the present or the unknowable future. So what could I do? What can a dad do to fix a mess as deep and dirty as this?

Even though the immediate danger had passed, Bethany was far from being whole. Her life had been devastated, and our world had been turned upside down. I was becoming more and more aware that during much of the upcoming process of recovery, I would only be an observer. My role would need to shift from Bethany's physical protec-tor and provider to an alert and attentive spiritual leader. After all, the real tragedy, the real danger was not from without but from within.

We needed help.

We needed help for Bethany's mental and emotional loss, and we needed help for our family as a whole. We were in uncharted territory without any previous personal experiences to draw from. Paige and I felt alone, weary, and bewildered as to what to do next. Paige wanted to react and fix it right away: take Bethany out of school, get counseling, talk to the principal about confronting the boy—anything that would make her believe she was doing something concrete to take this awful circumstance away.

Finding help was not as simple as just calling a 1-800 number and being assigned a professional family advisor. It wasn't going to be easy for us to sit down with our small group at church and start spewing our emotional guts all over everyone for prayer. I mean, this was painful, embarrassing stuff, and it was really awkward. It would not do just to lay this issue of ours out for mass consumption, even with those in our church who were fellow believers in Christ.

Paige and I began to pray about what would be healthiest for Bethany. We took her to see a Christian psychologist and our family pediatrician, and as it turned out, that was exactly what she needed. We discovered that Bethany would need to process this mentally and spiritually in her own time and in her own way. But in the interim we needed to provide her with the structure and support of a healthy home and the unrestrained love of her parents. No, we didn't get an immediate solution for our daughter. No pill or sixty-minute weekly counseling session was going to be able to repair all the things that had gone wrong, and we would not be finding any quick fixes or simple solutions. But we did take comfort in knowing that at least we were on some kind of path forward.

We briefly considered taking Bethany out of her freshman year of high school to be homeschooled, but in the end we had no peace about it. We met with the school principal and considered pursuing legal claims against the young man who had caused the whole episode, but when we were advised strongly against doing so for Bethany's mental and emotional sake, we reluctantly agreed. It would take time, a large and persistent investment of prayer, ongoing Christian counseling, and some prudent medication, but slowly Bethany began to come back to us. And as her world began to right itself, so did ours.

In hindsight it's obvious that God was already at work in our family, even in the very earliest days of this crisis. After a few weeks of medical attention and counseling, we all began to see the slow improvement in our daughter—changed attitudes, brighter eyes, and even some joy in her smile as life slowly came back into her. It was not easy, and it was not simple . . . but it was happening. Bethany's shame about what had happened to her had lifted after our time of prayer, and she had started to read her Bible again regularly. Her interest in food, school, and our family returned, but her guarded looks and flares of anger and irritation remained.

As we slowly recovered, I remembered one of my father's sayings. He always asserted that each difficult life circumstance was used by God to teach us valuable life lessons that we could only learn in the midst of crisis. So I asked God to show me whatever it was I was supposed to be learning from all this—and then settled back to hear his answer. I had no idea how right my dad was and how much God would have to say.

Insight

My first major breakthrough came in January 2010. I took a brief trip into the Colorado wilderness, and there I experienced a significant shift in my understanding of God, my life, and Bethany. This was later cemented by a powerful book I read by Francis Chan titled *Crazy Love*.

At the time, I was pursuing a new role in church leadership. Today I am actively involved with ministry and have been for several years, initially as a small group leader in our local church and now as an associate pastor in the final stages of ordination. During this process I attended some rigorous seminary courses in theology, apologetics, biblical history, and psychology, all with the intention of using them for God later in my life. Another important part of my preparation included embracing the Word of God as a daily devotion. In fact, that daily reading commitment grew into spiritual retreats with my best friend and ministry partner, Brian Hardin. He and I began taking road trips several times each year into the mountains of Colorado, Appalachia, Utah, Wyoming, Montana, California, Oregon, Washington, and Arizona. One of those road trips was in January 2010.

Our media and business trips allowed us to travel frequently. If we were going anywhere near a mountain range or national wilderness area, we took full advantage—and each time we drove with the Word of God open on the seat between us. On our trips we read faithfully together from the daily Scripture text. I usually drove, while Brian read aloud from my beat-up copy of *The One Year Bible*. We soaked up the beauty of God with our eyes and the truth of God with our ears. That divine wisdom would gradually seep into our hearts and change us both. Brian was, is, and by God's grace forever shall remain my comrade. In his quiet and careful way, he led me in the midst of my pain to consider reading Chan's book.

Crazy Love was powerful—not because its ideas were so revolutionary, but because it brought me back to the core of my Christian faith. It reminded me of the deepest truth behind our relationship with God and the strongest weapon any of us could possibly have in our spiritual lives: *love*. Chan's book illustrated the power every Christian could experience from living every day motivated by love.

I needed that book more than I ever could have imagined, and God used it to begin a process of reconfiguring many erroneous beliefs I had about him. *Crazy Love* so radically affected my perspective on faith, ministry, and life that it immediately began to impact my home, my marriage, and the attitudes I had about being a parent.

Did I say *radically affected*? I meant to say transformed—totally, completely, undeniably, indescribably, indefinably changed in every molecule of my understanding of life. It basically rewrote my beliefs about my kids and my family—beliefs I didn't realize I had been holding on to so tightly, creating unhealthy attitudes that had been quietly undermining my whole life.

Chan's book helped me realize that God wanted me to *love* him, not cringe from him. From the time I was a kid, I'd been afraid of God, and so I frequently avoided him for fear of his wrath or displeasure. But once I realized how intense God's love is, that fear didn't make sense anymore. I wanted to live differently now, not anxious and burdened by my own guilt and shame, but genuinely desiring to be with him, to seek him out, and to enjoy his presence whenever I could. Not because of what he could bless me with, or solve, fix, or remove from my life, but out of a sincere and desperate affection for being in the presence of my heavenly Father.

This was new stuff for me—not intellectually, but in my heart. Brand-new. It was freeing.

I know, I know . . . everybody learned this basic building block of faith in Sunday school. My family made it to church every Sunday, and we learned it hundreds of times from our pastors, from our hymns and weekly worship songs, from the picture books of the Bible. We preached God's love as the "Good News," we taught Jesus as the "the Way, the Truth, and the Life," and we pounded the memory verses from Scripture into our heads. But until that love seeps into the inner recesses of our hearts, it doesn't change us. It hadn't changed me until this crisis.

I realized that I had been parenting with the goal of "getting it right." I would go through my own mental checklist of how to be a good father: Work hard to spend the right amount of time with my kids? Check. Do daddy-daughter dates every third Saturday? Check. Give my kids new clothes and plenty of food? Check. Make sure they get proper sleep, do their homework and chores, and act polite in public? Check. Paige and I had been doing the "right" things as Bethany's parents, but something vital had been missing: love.

All my fathering attentions were based on my own fear of messing up their lives, of not living up to my role. I loved my kids, but the driving force in my relationship with them was fear, not compassion or grace or patience. For example, my teenage daughters were quick to hide their emotional interests in boys. It was a huge source of anxiety for me, and I was constantly warning them about the danger of letting their hearts get broken by a premature crush on a young man who was not ready for a serious relationship. Unfortunately, I created the very situation I was hoping to avoid. Because I constantly showed my displeasure with my girls calling, texting, or hanging out with young men, I was reinforcing their belief that I would never allow them to go out on a date. As a result, they never willingly told me about a boyfriend. They hid the truth about their relationships, and when I found out, I would overreact and blast into them about not being honest with me. That of course was true, but it was due mostly to my own fears intruding on reality. It was a selfish and un-settled way of parenting, and it had not worked out well. In my rush to do the right things as a father, I had forgotten to consider the *why*.

On a conceptual level, I knew that God loved my children deeply. But on a heart level, I forgot that he cares for them even more than I do. I got caught up with informing my kids *about* Christianity, about proper beliefs, about our family values, about God and the Scriptures and the need for their lives to be submitted to his will. I had that part nailed. Yet I was so focused on preparing my kids to understand God, faith, and our beliefs that I had forgotten to show them how my personal relationship with God worked. I had forgotten to introduce them to the vast, overwhelming love God has for them. I had externalized my faith, spending all my energy educating my kids to know facts about God, rather than sharing with them the incredible reality of who he is. I was trying to cram my faith into their *heads* when all that really mattered was what got in their *hearts*.

I had missed the real target, mostly because I had been aiming at a worthless goal—creating a socially acceptable, outwardly compliant child rather than directing my kids to God himself, who could change them from the inside out. I had taken the burden of my family's spiritual transformation from God and filtered it through my anal personality.

My basic failure wasn't in the time or effort I had given my family but in the ways that I had spent that time. I'd failed to absorb the most important truths about God, and that lack of wisdom proved costly. It allowed my anxious motivation to shift from winning my children's hearts to controlling their behavior in a "get it right" approach. For myself and for my children, God wanted me to grasp the truth about a life motivated by love.

Why am I spending so much time explaining my epiphany about God's love? Because this point is critical. Because I am Bethany's earthly father, the beliefs, attitudes, and perspectives I have about my heavenly Father will inevitably impact her. Good or bad, I am her representation of God the Father in the flesh. And in my misunderstanding of God's character, I had indirectly taught her to fear disappointing her earthly father above all else . . . so much so that it almost cost us her life. She was more concerned about disappointing me than about enduring the shame of her painful secrets alone. How many of us fathers make the same mistake? My sense is that there are many millions of dads who fall into the same trap I did.

If you're a father and this is making you feel a bit uncomfortable, stop reading. Take a few minutes right now to pray and honestly ask God if this is something you might be in danger of repeating in your own family.

Love Leads the Way

> If I speak with human eloquence and angelic ecstasy but don't love, I'm nothing but the creaking of a rusty gate. If I speak God's Word with power, revealing all his mysteries and making everything plain as day, and if I have faith that says to a mountain, "Jump," and it jumps, but I don't love, I'm nothing. If I give everything I own to the poor and even go to the stake to be burned as a martyr, but I don't love, I've gotten nowhere. So, no matter what I say, what I believe, and what I do, I'm bankrupt without love. (1 Corinthians 13:1-3, *The Message*)

My personal growth and understanding about God, his character, his love, and my motivations would go on to dramatically affect my own fathering traits. To quote A. W. Tozer's classic book *The Knowledge of the Holy*, "What comes into our minds when we think about God is the most important thing about us. . . . Worship is pure or base as the worshiper entertains high or low thoughts of God. For this reason the gravest question before the Church is always God Himself, and the most portentous fact about any man is not what he at a given time may say or do, but what he in his deep heart conceives God to be like."[1]

This growing understanding of God's true character and compassionate nature would soften my tone, my posture, and my entire perspective on leading at work, in ministry, and in my own home. It would free me to redirect damaging old habits into new healthier ones. It would change how I would respond to life's twists and turns. I found myself wanting to understand the reason my daughter was being belligerent to me or her siblings. Rather than just correcting her or angrily confronting the behaviors, I wanted to understand *why* she was acting the way she was. It became more important for me to grasp what was motivating her actions, rather than simply reacting to them. This desire to look beyond the surface and see the heart behind the life came from my new understanding of the nature of God.

Most of our lives have not really been built upon a foundation of love; instead we are weakly anchored to a flimsy raft called worry. We find ourselves drifting around life, helpless against a relentless current. Waves of fear constantly threaten to capsize us. We struggle to float along in our leaky little raft. Every so often, we futilely attempt to blow some more air into our weak plastic vessel, never noticing the deadly tidal wave directly ahead. It rarely occurs to us that with Christ in our lives, we have the option of getting out of the sinking raft and walking on the water—across the waves of fear and onto the safe, dry ground of love.

In our ignorance as parents, we often have settled for something less than God's best plans for our lives. We've co-opted the readily available love of God for the comfort of our self-satisfying legalistic structures and personal disciplines. Unknowingly, I had misled my family to do the same. I was really only intent on playing defense, attempting to remake my kids into my own image, rather than letting God mold them into his. My fear gave me an unhealthy need to retain control in my home. When things got out of hand, I held on even tighter, which only made things worse. Ultimately the whole cycle was fueled by my lack of understanding about God, his love, and my kids' divine purpose.

When I read *Crazy Love*, I knew that God had provided me with a powerful key, a life principle vital to unlocking the door to my daughter's heart and my family's recovery. The key was love, and its simple but profound influence on my life was enough to begin the process of healing. I knew that, in time, it had the potential to resolve every painful, convoluted issue our family was struggling with and restore every loss we had endured. The problem was that I didn't really grasp love's power, much less how to allow its presence to fill my heart, my mind, and ultimately my home. I had been a Christian for almost eight years, but I was still a newborn baby when it came to understanding my God.

Dealing with Dad—from the Top Down and Inside Out

I prayed faithfully for God to continue to heal my daughter's wounds, but Bethany still struggled with her identity and confidence, despite the praying and counseling and medications. I was anxious for my daughter to become whole again, for God to ease her pain and heal her spirit. But as I kept praying for him to change my daughter, to my surprise he began to change me instead.

So far, God's primary means to Bethany's healing wasn't in showing us a better parenting approach or a hip new style of communication. It wasn't in helping us find a well-respected Christian counseling center. Rather, it seemed that *God was investing in a total makeover of me.*

I had said I was willing to do whatever it took, that I was totally committed to making whatever changes in our home were necessary to help my daughter. But to my embarrassment, the changes God wanted were not concerned with others; they were specific to me.

God was acting to change the leader, the head of the home, first. He never wavered; he never hesitated at all. He acted, and he started the healing with me. I was stunned. It was weird, it was humbling, and it was very unexpected. It had to be God.

It's often easier to see God's pattern in our lives from a distance—that's why it can be obvious to others but not to us personally. That sure was the case with me. God began actively healing our daughter through a deep and defining reconciliation in me. The problems in my home were being fueled largely by my own immaturity and pride, and any actions that I might attempt to help Bethany would be doomed to failure if I didn't allow God to rearrange my heart in preparation for healing hers.

I was finally starting to get the message: I needed to trade my fear-based parenting and reactionary living for an intentional life motivated by love. When I shared these ideas with Paige, she had a lightbulb moment as she realized the truth in it for herself as well. She had never thought about it before, but her parenting style had been based on fear too.

Many of our daughter's problems were by-products of our need to be in control and to push her—rather than lead her—into adulthood. I had not realized how prevalent the fear of failure, of disappointing God, was in our lives, and it had almost cost our daughter hers. How could I ever teach my kids about following God out of love without experiencing it firsthand for myself? The answer was . . . I couldn't. No one can.

THREE

PARENT GUILT AND PARENT PAIN

Do not be fooled into thinking the transformational journey is necessarily a smooth, predictable, linear, or progressive adventure. . . . Most believers are stunned by how long and arduous the journey to wholeness is. And if you were hoping that the route to wholeness would be one of familiarity and serenity, think again. Every believer who doggedly pursues transformation with God will spend oodles of time outside of their comfort zone—emotionally, intellectually, spiritually, relationally, and behaviorally.

GEORGE BARNA, *MAXIMUM FAITH*

WITH THE ESSENTIAL UNDERSTANDING now fresh in mind that I needed to live my life motivated by love, not fear, I was beginning to allow a much-needed change in my parenting habits. However, such

newly acquired knowledge did not immediately resolve the deeper
pain and problems of the past. Yes, a better future was beginning to
take shape in my mind and heart, but in the here and now of life,
things were not all that different. Before we could move forward,
Paige and I would have to deal with three significant and deeply
ingrained issues: struggling with our pride, finding purpose in our
pain, and learning to let go of our guilt.

Parent Pride

My wife and I slowly worked out practical steps to help Bethany
cope with her mood swings and occasional bouts of depression. In
time, we started to believe that our daughter was going to recover,
and maybe so would we. However, our previous personal pride as her
parents had mostly evaporated in the shadow of accepting our role in
her collapse. When that pride and confidence left us, it took along
with it our faith in our parenting abilities. We no longer assumed we
had what it takes to successfully prepare our kids for adulthood. We
were running on empty, with nothing left to give. Maybe someday
we could recover our confidence enough to give our children at least
a running head start, some semblance of wise counsel to direct their
emotional maturity and spiritual balance—but that was iffy at best.
In the weeks and months following Bethany's crisis, Paige and I wondered aloud between ourselves if God was still going to be able to use
us effectively in her life.

As parents, our self-assurance had been wiped away. We were left
feeling inadequate and alone, filled with the dull ache of just how
badly we had misunderstood Bethany's condition. We had tried to be
good parents. We spent lots of personal time with her. We took her
shopping, bought her gifts, made sure she had healthy friendships and
attended church regularly, and had sent her to summer camp the year

before. And we had done our part too—we dutifully attended the parenting courses at church; Paige had read at least a dozen Christian authors on the subject of parenting girls; and we thought we had been dutifully attentive to the circumstances of our kids' lives. Realizing just how badly our efforts had fallen short filled us with shock and guilt. Not only were we forced to accept that our parenting strategies were inept, but we had to acknowledge that the how-to books didn't seem to give us any real help in resolving things on our own.

We were unsure of our next steps. I was trying to use my fresh understanding of God to live out a love-motivated life, but I was still fearful of messing things up even worse than before. I knew all too well how my personality would often attach itself to new ideas or concepts and ferociously embrace them for a while, only to abandon them later when I grew bored. What if this Love vs. Fear concept was just another fad, a transient spiritual awakening for my personal distraction and consumption? I was determined not to proceed until I knew that God was directing us to do so, but that left us in sort of a parenting stalemate. At the same time, Paige was depending on me to encourage her and to share what God was showing me about Bethany and how best to parent her. As a result, my wife was learning to apply the same lens of truth to her own heart and actions as a mother.

Our home life seemed to be stabilizing, and we both seemed to be more aware of Bethany's needs. What else could we do to help our daughter? We needed support, encouragement, and a wise outside perspective. But where could we get it? We didn't know a single parent or family who had walked down this road before. If we opened up about our situation, we would be the first of our band of friends to reveal a significant problem with a child. It was daunting to admit our failure publicly among our peers and then stoop to asking for help from those who had previously held us in such high esteem. Our pride was holding us back.

As God had forced me years ago to become authentic in my personal behavior, he was now interested in seeing us as parents do the same. He wanted us to match our actions with our words, to put hands and feet to our parenting faith. It was uncomfortable, it was embarrassing, and it was heading us straight into uncharted territory.

But we did it.

We humbled ourselves and took some giant leaps of faith. We confided in our parents and in a few couples from church we had learned to trust over the years. Although we struggled with that decision, in the end we admitted that this was too much to carry on our own. We had found some major gaps in our understanding about God, love, fear, and life. Our parenting practices had been adequate by most Christian standards, but in reality we had "majored in the minors," and our ultimate goal of raising our kids well was now seriously in doubt. Maybe sharing our frustrations and fears with other parents would provide us with the insight we were missing.

Sharing your parenting failure with your own mother and father is a huge step. It means admitting that you couldn't do what they did without help. But what most of us don't realize is how much our parents understand and can truly sympathize. In most cases, no one knows us or our kids better than our own parents do, so listening to their counsel and input is an essential step forward. No matter how messy your personal relationships may still be with your own parents, stepparents, or grandparents, don't skip sharing with them. The wisdom and influence they exert over your life both socially and spiritually cannot be overstated and remains a largely untapped resource for many parents in crisis.

We were surprised at the strength our parents showed when we shared our plight regarding Bethany. They strongly encouraged us to stay the course and trust in the power of God to keep us on the right path as parents. At that critical moment we needed their affirmation, their support, and their unwavering faith that things would indeed work out. They gave us that perspective of hope, at a time when all we could see and feel was darkness.

It also turned out that sharing our pain with fellow Christian parents was, surprisingly, not so bad. We hadn't counted on the amazing capacity Christians have to offer genuine encouragement and advice in times of great stress or crisis. Our friends were on our side and assured us they would do anything they could to help, and their prayerful support was incredibly powerful.

Once we swallowed our pride and made the effort to confide in others, things didn't immediately change. Paige and I were not suddenly full of confidence and optimism about Bethany's recovery, but we knew that we were no longer carrying this burden on our own. We had help, and we had support. Breaking that mental and emotional isolation was a key factor in our coming to grips with the true circumstances of our situation.

Fear, doubt, and shame can rob us of our ability to see our lives clearly. We see bigger obstacles, darker shadows, and weaker lights than what may actually be present, and our emotional reactions can keep us from acting on our spiritual instincts. We need the ability to review ideas, impressions, and options with faithful Christian couples who can objectively speak truth to us. For Paige and me, that accountability was an essential tether to hold us to our faith and our community. It also provided us with prayer support and affirmation—two things we desperately needed.

Our friends and family provided refreshment to our spirits when we were exhausted. Their love kept a prayer covering over our lives and aided us in a way that we will never fully understand. But when we agreed to ask for help, we won a significant battle. We had defeated our tendency as parents to isolate ourselves and handle things on our own. We had broken down our pride, and in its absence we were freed for the journey ahead.

There's a well-known saying in church circles, repeated by so many pastors and teachers that I have no idea whose wisdom it was originally: "You can go faster on your own, but you can go further with others." Paige and I found this to be true. The only catch is that you have to step forward in humility, without reservations or conditions, to find out.

Parent Pain

Any parent who has walked through an ordeal like ours knows that the greater challenge isn't necessarily in surviving the crisis, or the immediate days afterward, but in enduring the long-term struggle of moving forward together. So it was with us.

For many couples who live through a serious family crisis or lose a child, their relationship itself barely survives the process. More commonly, couples deal with the emotional and psychological trauma by creating a relational wall between them in an effort to avoid their pain and guilt. In time, each withdraws further and further from the other, as the need to isolate wins out over the need couples have to share life as partners. The marriage may be technically intact, but the relationship is severed. The single tragedy becomes greater, its impact more profound, and the isolated loss becomes a slow-moving avalanche, multiplying misery and pain as it sweeps through the home and continues its dark destruction. This was a serious risk for us.

By God's grace, this did not happen.

I'm sure my marriage would have become another statistic without our collective community of faith, as well as our growing humility and personal understanding of just how much we truly needed God to guide our family into the future. Through the aftermath of Bethany's molestation and near suicide, I never doubted our commitment to each other, but I did wonder how much pain it would continue to cause in our home and our marriage. It seemed that our entire household was nervous, taut with anxious concern, always looking closely at Bethany's wrists or eyes for any hint of continuing danger to her life.

The tension affected our other two kids. I remember many days when Jessica would turn around whenever Bethany came into a room, leaving as quickly as she could. She was desperate to avoid any more confrontations or arguments with her sister. Often Bethany had asked Jessica to lie for her or help her meet up with a boy by telling us she was somewhere else. Jessica couldn't take it anymore. Caleb was withdrawn around Bethany and often would just stare angrily at her for treating him so rudely. I would find them furiously disagreeing in the kitchen, usually about who had eaten the last of the Goldfish crackers or ice cream. Usually it ended with Caleb retreating upstairs to his own room for some peace and quiet.

Paige and I were old marital survivors, and yet we were dangerously close to drowning in our own pain, afraid to admit out loud our inner doubts and fears. Gradually we allowed our carefully preserved facade—the mature and healthy couple who "had it all together"—to crumble. Our energies were no longer being focused outwardly, but inwardly. We were done with the need to project to our little community the lie that we had our parenting ducks in a row. But the pain of past regrets and the growing presence of volatile anger were lurking just below the surface for each of us. We still wanted to find someone to blame, someone to accuse.

My pride was strong enough to tempt me to deny that I had played any real role in the problem. Bethany's crisis must have been caused by hormones—or the rapidly devolving morality outside our door. At times I was sure the blame should lie, at least in part, with my wife for lacking the maternal intuition to sense Bethany's misery, or with my parents for teaching me to be so firm and confrontational with issues in my kids' lives. I wondered if the church itself had failed me and taught me inaccurate principles of raising my kids, or if the problem was due to my overcommitments to work and ministry. It didn't stop there. I kept looking to assign blame wherever I could imagine it, even though I had no real idea who or what was responsible. Maybe it was an "all of the above" kind of answer. Not one factor, but everything combined.

I started to realize that some of the blame could be laid at my own feet because of my past failings as a leader. For most of my married life, I had acted and Paige had followed. When things troubled her, or she disagreed with me on anything important, I would either talk her out of it, refuse to admit her point, or explode in frustration and anger until she stopped resisting. That bled over into parenting choices as well. When the kids were young, I set the boundaries and enforced the consequences, paying little attention to Paige's point of view.

She put up with a significant amount of my solo parenting style for years, until after our "almost divorce" when I went to the other extreme and let her take over with the kids. I had been absent for months, and I didn't feel I had any moral authority. I felt so guilty for my failure to be faithful that I didn't know how to step into a clear leadership role with my kids. After my life had changed, when I became a genuinely transformed man, I should have taken up my role and become the spiritual leader in our home. But the truth was that

I was content to stay where I was, on the sidelines. I allowed myself to be passive and disengaged.

If Paige wanted the kids to do chores, I let her manage that part of our home. If she felt the kids needed to do more homework or watch less television, I let her make that decision too. My primary role in our family was reduced to providing food, clothing, and shelter. I understood that I needed to be ready to step up as a healthy role model, a stable parent, and a father figure. But in the bigger picture I was more than happy to play only a support role in the kids' discipline and everyday problems.

My passive approach to parenting had allowed me to entrust everything to my wife when it came to our kids. If she was at peace, then I was at peace. On the day-to-day issues I always deferred to her. But if the kids did something that affected me or my stuff, I suddenly stepped in—and often overreacted.

Since I've become a pastor, this is a pattern I've seen over and over as I've counseled parents. A dad might let his wife handle all the messy everyday parenting chores, but pity the kids who leave a mess in Dad's car or forget to return a tool they borrowed. If they're guilty of denting the family car and not telling him, or spending money on things he considers frivolous—look out. The bottom line is that the father can easily become a passive-aggressive leader who creates an unhealthy atmosphere of instability in the home. His wife and kids are left walking on eggshells, unsure of what will set him off and anxious to avoid the smallest of infractions that might annoy him. The result is a culture of tension and fear.

This dysfunctional system of parenting is common, but that does not make it right. If I was looking for someone to blame, I couldn't exclude myself: Some of our current pain was based in my past failure to lead at home by serving and loving my family as a dad should. I had neglected the role God had designed me to fill, and it had cost my family.

My lack of leadership extended into other areas too. I was personally a very faithful daily reader of the Word, and I spent regular time in prayer alone with God. But it felt a bit awkward for Paige and me to do these things together. Our prayer life as a couple was sporadic at best. I regret that dearly. We were too busy, or we were too tired, or it was difficult to find the desire to pray—so most evenings, we avoided it. It was unusual for us both to be in bed at the same time at night and have enough energy left even to talk, let alone pray about our kids. Instead we sought God on our own and occasionally shared with each other what we might be sensing about the kids, our lives, or the future. When Bethany's crisis exploded, that changed.

One night Paige and I began to talk about our situation in earnest. She admitted her personal determination to be the best mom possible, to get it "right," to carry out a Betty Crocker life while sustaining a nine-to-five career. That's what she thought a good mom was. Her expectations of marriage and motherhood were incredibly high, and her hopes and dreams for having a happy home were now in pieces. She was in pain, hurting over what seemed to be one of her greatest failures. The one and only thing she had desperately clung to in the past decade had been her ability to be a great mom, and now that accomplishment seemed on the verge of disintegrating.

Paige had survived her own painful childhood trauma with the divorce of her parents when she was very young, and the resultant ever-so-common social awkwardness of living in a blended stepfamily as a teen. From her earliest years, she had struggled with the fear of never being able to fully integrate her life into another's, and that stress stayed with her well into college and our marriage. As a child, she had hated being uprooted when circumstances forced her family to move, and as an adult, she battled the nagging feeling that she belonged nowhere. We had moved a lot, and I knew she felt the strain of constantly needing to start over, to reestablish her home and her relationships in yet another new and unfamiliar neighborhood, state, or school. Nothing could have been more essential, more valuable to my wife than real stability in the home. She had craved it her whole life and sought diligently to prevent harmful family crises from harming our kids' lives as they had hers. But even that effort had not been enough to protect Bethany, and now Paige was blaming herself.

Of course, we had already been through some very dark times as individuals and as a couple, and God had come through for us. But this problem was different from our "almost divorce." It was our daughter's battle—so close to us, yet so completely out of our hands. Our marital tsunami years were as traumatic as anyone's, but in that crisis, Paige and I had, to some degree, the individual control to influence an outcome. Not so with Bethany. This was on her. We couldn't change the way she felt about herself, God, or us. We couldn't recover her innocence and joy and hope; only she could. We could encourage her, support her, and spend time with her, but in the end the details were out of our hands.

It was scary and frustrating to be so close and yet so far away. Bethany wasn't running back to us like the little girl we had raised. She wasn't excited to pursue God or faith or healthy friendships. She was basically still centering her life around her external appearance and popularity, more concerned about people finding out about her situation than with how close she had come to irreversible harm. She didn't want to talk about her feelings anymore; she didn't want us to check her wrists and arms for marks; she didn't like being watched by everyone for the slightest hint of mental instability—in fact, she resented it and stepped back a little from our love. That was incredibly painful for us to endure.

When your child is still under your roof yet becomes so emotionally distant, so removed from your life, a sort of panic begins to grow. Paige and I had a feeling that no matter what we did, it wouldn't be enough to help her. We experienced a growing sensation of hopelessness, regret, and guilt that Bethany had been hurt because we had not done the right things at the right times. We became victims of the what-if game. What if we hadn't read the best books? What if we hadn't prayed enough with her at night? What if we should have taken her to more Sunday school classes or done family devotions more consistently? What if we should have homeschooled her and simplified our lives so Paige could become a stay-at-home mom? The list was endless, detailed, and gut-wrenching.

Bethany still had a mountain of pain in her own heart. She felt the deep pain of rejection, the pain of being different, the pain of guilt for being attractive to boys and somehow bringing this entire terrible event upon herself. She struggled with the fear of disappointing her mother and me, of not living up to our expectations and her own. She lived with the pain of feeling fat or ugly, of not having the best hair and makeup, of wearing out-of-date clothes . . . you name it, she was struggling with it. Some of it was typical teen angst, and some of it was not. The trick was helping her to sort out the normal, growing-up pain from the abnormal.

Paige was suffering, I was suffering, and our daughter was suffering. We had no idea how to relieve the pain or whom to blame. As parents, we struggled with the knowledge that we had not only failed our daughter in the past, but it was a distinct possibility we were still failing her now. God seemed far away, and any hope for a return to "normal" was quickly fading from view. We had reached an uneasy equilibrium of sorts, a tenuous status quo for our home. It was our emotional version of "don't ask, don't tell," and to some degree, it was working. But the pain remained, and the blame never seemed to be resolved.

Finding Purpose in the Pain

As the weeks passed into months, our pain slowly started to fade. Paige and I gradually began to recognize that God wanted us to acknowledge our concerns and not sweep them under the rug anymore. We also needed to let go of the blame question. The various sources of our pain were not the real issue; the bigger picture had been our decision to ignore our problems, to choose not to respond at all.

Emotional pain, just like physical pain, serves a valuable purpose: to warn of danger and potential harm. If we ignore this alarm or choose to mask it with painkillers, we run the risk of irreparable damage or even death. God was allowing us to see and feel the pain in our home afresh. He was reminding us not to ignore it any longer and to seek out a thorough reconciliation for those issues that had yet to be healed.

I remember speaking often about our growing understanding of God's love for us as our heavenly Father. He wouldn't allow us to hide from him anymore. Although it was painful, he was showing his love for us by forcing us to confront these issues and march forward instead of retreating. The pain was serving a much healthier purpose as it caused us to begin to change. We couldn't afford to remain the same, and this uncomfortable trial was leading us out of our frustrated past into a hopeful future. One passage that encouraged us during this journey was Hebrews 12:5-13 (NLT):

> Have you forgotten the encouraging words God spoke to
> you as his children? He said,

ROAD TRIP TO REDEMPTION

"My child, don't make light of the LORD's discipline, and
don't give up when he corrects you. For the LORD disciplines
those he loves, and he punishes each one he accepts as his
child."

As you endure this divine discipline, remember that
God is treating you as his own children. Who ever heard
of a child who is never disciplined by its father? If God
doesn't discipline you as he does all of his children, it means
that you are illegitimate and are not really his children at
all. Since we respected our earthly fathers who disciplined
us, shouldn't we submit even more to the discipline of the
Father of our spirits, and live forever?

For our earthly fathers disciplined us for a few years,
doing the best they knew how. But God's discipline is always
good for us, so that we might share in his holiness. No
discipline is enjoyable while it is happening—it's painful!
But afterward there will be a peaceful harvest of right living
for those who are trained in this way.

So take a new grip with your tired hands and strengthen
your weak knees. Mark out a straight path for your feet so that
those who are weak and lame will not fall but become strong.

A critical step in the recovery process was now engaged. Denial
was on the run, and our pain began to serve a much healthier purpose
in our lives. However, we still had one more barrier in our road to
healing: guilt.

Parent Guilt

In the core of my soul, I had believed a lie—a terrible half-truth
about God that had slowly eroded my understanding of his nature,

moving me away from the freedom that grace gives and into the bondage that self-righteous deception ensures. *I had believed I could earn God's favor with my own efforts.* Deep down I felt that the act of praying a sinner's prayer and accepting the offer of salvation was just the entrance exam for Christians. It was a starting point for infant believers pursuing their larger goal of gaining full and true redemption, a preschool program designed to train us until we made it into the lifelong University of Self-Righteousness.

That philosophy works great if your religious life is moving along at a predictably healthy clip and all is well in your home and church. It's not so great to hold on to when your family starts to implode. After all that had gone wrong in my life and our home, I was sure that God shouldn't, couldn't, and wouldn't be able to accept me or my feeble efforts. If I couldn't figure out this faith and family stuff by myself, and at the very least ensure that my own flesh and blood would follow in my footsteps, then I was sure I had *no* chance of regaining God's favor, blessing, and help. I was desperate to figure out what I could do to make things better for us all. What could I pledge to God to fix this mess? How much would I need to give up to gain his favor again? But I was feeling the pinch of not having anything valuable enough left to bargain with.

I was learning about love, humility, and the purpose of pain, but I had yet to learn about the power of guilt to deceive my heart.

A powerful burden of self-condemnation plagues many Christian parents. When we expect to soar above the pagan masses and become superhuman examples of faithfulness and exemplary lifestyles, we're setting ourselves up for failure. Consciously or not, we believe that if we do everything right with our kids, we can live without the struggles that other people have—or at the very least, earn our way closer to God. When life doesn't work out that way, we are plagued by guilt.

I had carried my burden of guilt and false superiority with me from childhood to adulthood, and over time it had permeated every facet of my life. It had directed my authoritarian nature and achievement-based mentality, as well as the physical expressions and postures I took with my wife and kids when I corrected them. I sought out a legalistic philosophy and pattern of ministry. Guilt is very compatible with legalism, so that mind-set felt comfortable and natural to me.

All those facets came together and collapsed on top of me when I realized that my daughter's life could have ended that tragic night. In a moment, a lifetime of falsely held convictions about God was stripped away. In its place there was only a vast sea of guilt, shame, and failure.

Guilt eats many Christians alive, even without the added burden of a family tragedy like ours to complicate the issue. If left unchecked, guilt destroys marriages and homes with a surprisingly predictable ease. Like a deadly virus, it replicates itself and spreads from the mind and heart to overcome the whole body and the spirit of a home. It contaminates every cell, every molecule of one's life, relentlessly invading every peaceful and contented thought one can muster, crushing them with its critical sting.

Guilt destroys grace and peace; it pushes back joy and hope like a massive broom as it sweeps the very spirit of God out of our presence. It refocuses the mind on the personal and fleshly, avoiding the spiritual and heavenly. Guilt removes the bedrock of our salvation—and replaces it with a devastating pseudo-truth that we lean on in place of true faith. For the sake of this discussion, we will call it *earned faith*.

The temptation to trust our "earned faith" is not a new problem for believers; Paul spoke against it to the early church in almost every epistle he penned. In reality, our salvation is not about anything we bring to the table. Yet for us hardworking religious folks to have no edge over those almost-pagans who mess up their lives over and over again—well, that irritates us to no end. It just doesn't seem fair that we don't get any credit for all our efforts. We don't like the ultimate grace concept because it excludes us from having anything to contribute. As new believers in Christ, we have only gratitude, humility, and childlike joy. But if we're "earned faith" parents, we need a bit more. We accept our need for a Savior, but we qualify it with a belief that our spiritual poverty is less than others', that they need Jesus more than we do. This basic lie is buried deeply in the foundation of our hearts and minds, even if we don't speak of it aloud.

The lie of "earned faith" can lie dormant for years, decades in fact, slowly building its presumption into a core belief that we begin to trust. It overshadows our childlike acceptance of grace, love, and redemption. Those earlier beliefs quickly evaporate in our need to have a role—any role—in the great story of our lives. We can't accept that the simple words of Scripture are for us; those are for the less initiated, the less educated, the less mature Christians.

Wow, that's some pretty serious garbage. When you actually articulate "earned faith" as a principle or belief, it quickly reveals itself for what it really is. Call it what you want—filth, refuse, blasphemy—it has no place in our hearts or our homes. But when we let it in, guilt is not far behind.

Legalism was a part of my earliest education about God, so I easily accepted those lies about myself, and they stuck. Inside of me they formed a root of deep deception that would reach out over thirty years later and almost destroy my life, my marriage, and my daughter. I infected my home with the subtle belief that our kids were better than other families' kids. That our standards should be higher and that our lives should be cleaner, healthier, and holier. This lie implied to my children that if they were good, God would bless them out of respect for their hard work and dedication rather than out of his heart of love and grace. And if they didn't live up to our standards . . . well, that's where the guilt comes in.

As Paige and I processed our pride and pain as parents individually and then together, it became clear that she blamed herself and I blamed myself. Our guilt was self-incriminating and as devastating as if we had blamed each other. Paige felt she should have sensed earlier that something was wrong with her daughter. The burden of working full-time as a teacher and not being available to be with Bethany was suffocating my wife. At times she erupted in severe frustration, anger, and depression, lashing out at herself, me, her work, our church, her parents, my parents, you name it.

I, on the other hand, reverted to my childhood training about what I thought I knew about God and his ways. It wasn't fun to do. I was under a powerful weight of guilt as a failed father, but at a darker level of my soul I felt the pain of falling short and somehow disappointing God. I couldn't articulate exactly what I was feeling, but I sensed that my inability to fix this situation was due not to the circumstances around me but to my lack of wisdom, my lack of knowledge of who God really was. His nature and his character were now fuzzy in my mind. I was feeling so guilty that I really didn't want to spend time with him or read Scripture. My shame, my doubt, and my pain were driving me away from God—and to some degree, away from my marriage.

The guilt had to have a fertile field in which to grow. For me it was pride and presumption; for Paige it was fear and frustration. Yet we came to realize that guilt is not a healthy response to any parenting crisis, and in a Christian's heart, guilt is not a sign of God's presence. Conviction is God's way of spurring us to action; guilt is the devil's way of taking us out. We must not confuse the two.

As Paige and I began to run out of options to deal with our pride, our pain, and our guilt, we started to pray together. We sincerely wanted to move beyond the suffering and into some healing. We sought to find help, and in the process we rejected our pride and our "Christianity" for something simpler and more profound, something we commonly refer to as grace.

Guilt is powerless in the face of grace.

Now God has us where he wants us, with all the time in this world and the next to shower grace and kindness upon us in Christ Jesus. Saving is all his idea, and all his work. All we do is trust him enough to let him do it. It's God's gift from start to finish! We don't play the major role. If we did, we'd probably go around bragging that we'd done the whole thing! No, we neither make nor save ourselves. God does both the making and saving. He creates each of us by Christ Jesus to join him in the work he does, the good work he has gotten ready for us to do, work we had better be doing. (Ephesians 2:8, *The Message*)

It had never occurred to Paige or me that we might fail at raising our kids. We were both straight-A college students, high achievers, good problem solvers, and highly accomplished control freaks. But now, in the wake of this crisis, the evidence was undeniable. As parents, we had a lot to learn and many mistakes to correct. We had to make a choice: go forward with a critical spirit or one full of grace.

Grace comes into focus when we accept that we are powerless to change a thing. Grace allowed Paige and me to let go of our pride, pain, and guilt and accept God's forgiveness for our mistakes. This, in turn, allowed us to extend that same grace to each other as a family.

Grace eclipsed the power of fear, guilt, and shame, and it began to instill peace. We had confidence that God wasn't absent from our situation; in fact, he was in the midst of it, using something tragic to create something beautiful. Grace reminded us constantly that what we were in the midst of was not going to destroy us but bring us together. What started as a hope grew into a certainty that, although God never desired such tragedy for our daughter, he was going to use every bit of it to restore and redeem not only Bethany's identity but our family's as well.

As grace pushed out any residual shame and guilt, a subtle shift was beginning to occur in the Mathias home. Paige and I began to accept, even embrace the idea that we were not in control, that we didn't know how to parent our kids better than anyone else. It was actually a relief to admit our weakness. We found that in surrendering our perception of control to God, we grew more rested and secure.

God was reforming us all, realigning our spiritual spines, so speak. He was reformatting us to better absorb his life-changing truth, to be completely renewed. God was using a near disaster in our lives to help us discover these essential building blocks of truth, to help us believe with our hearts instead of our heads.

Moving Forward Together

Love and grace cannot be gained with intellectual observation, keen logic, or education. They only come as a by-product of our failure, exhaustion, and humility—and Paige and I had faced a lot of those in the last few months. Now, with our new, liberating understanding of grace, we were ready to move forward together.

Whatever solution God was going to provide, my wife and I would need to be in total agreement. I couldn't act solo on this parenting stuff any longer, and neither could Paige. God was not only redirecting my motivations and my understanding of grace but also helping me understand the need for my wife's total partnership. We couldn't plow ahead as individuals, each with our own set of issues, concerns, and priorities. We had to get on the same page and learn to support and love each other before we could ever hope to love and lead our family.

Before our time of crisis, I would have charged ahead in making the "big" decisions about our home or kids. After realizing just how inept I was as a leader, I realized how much I needed my wife by my side—not behind me. She had wisdom, grace, strength, and insight that I sorely lacked. She had to be a part of the solution. Without her input I would see only half of the whole picture, and I would be a fool to pretend otherwise.

I had seen God dismantle my carefully constructed, self-delusional, religious belief system in just a few months, and in doing so, he had reorganized and reprioritized my life. A huge part of our family's recovery would be built upon this new grace foundation.

I no longer believed I was a good parent. I no longer believed I had a great marriage. I no longer presumed that I had a clue about God and his character or his plan for our lives. I was being re-formed by God from the inside out, and that gave me both incredible humility and incredible hope. No longer would I (in the singular) seek to solve our problems. Instead, I would choose to seek God with my wife, and when we reached a unified course of action together, then and only then would I cautiously begin to act on that decision.

After struggles, pain, and discouragement, Paige and I emerged as Bethany's parents with a stronger, more unified faith in God. A faith that accepted the reality of grace being sufficient to cover us completely—including our failures, shortcomings, and fears. This renewed faith believed that God's plan would be so much better than our own, that someday our family would be whole again. It was a faith we found to be well placed. We were confident now that regardless of our abilities, efforts, or merit, God would show up.

FOUR

LEAVING THE OLD AND EMBRACING THE NEW

All great change in America begins at the dinner table.

RONALD REAGAN

WE KNEW GOD was with us. We had faith that he was still working in our lives and in Bethany's life. We were excited about what he was going to do! So we embraced a new goal: to raise children who could go against the grain, be themselves, understand grace, and pursue God with abandon. Yet, like many parents, we had times when we got discouraged because we couldn't see any progress. There were so many factors working against us, keeping us from connecting— media, technology, cultural attitudes toward Christianity. How could we overcome them all? Was there any life left in our daughter, in our family? Could she be revived not just to a shadow of her former self but to full life and strength?

In the Old Testament book of Ezekiel, we read about a similar challenge. The nation of Israel had to face a comparable threat to unity when they were exiled to Babylon after the fall of Jerusalem, almost six hundred years before the birth of Christ. An entire generation of Israelites were born and raised in the moral depravity of the Babylonian Empire, with little or no influence from the traditions, values, and beliefs of their forefathers. A new world was suddenly available to everyone, with untold vistas of wealth and excitement and opportunities. Babylon represented a new culture for the next generation of believers, one filled with fewer moral restrictions. This polytheistic society offered a wide variety of intellectual influences and entertainment options to be explored. There's no question the Israelites faced extreme culture shock, and parents likely watched in horror as their children veered further and further from the beliefs and behaviors they held dear.

In this setting of extreme cultural and societal transition and of dire moral collapse, God intervened by raising up great leaders— prophets like Daniel, Ezekiel, and Jeremiah. These men of integrity and faith were equipped by God to lead a recovery of their nation's values and beliefs in a turbulent time. They were tasked with the shepherding of God's remnant and with the responsibility of redirecting the Israelites' faith back to God. That's a heavy burden to carry in any generation!

In Ezekiel 37 we read about God showing the prophet Ezekiel a desert full of dry bones—a depressing sight. There was no hope at all in this scene, so Ezekiel must have been surprised when he was asked to prophesy the bones' resurrection from the grave.

The Lord took hold of me, and I was carried away by the
Spirit of the Lord to a valley filled with bones. He led me
all around among the bones that covered the valley floor.
They were scattered everywhere across the ground and were
completely dried out. Then he asked me, "Son of man, can
these bones become living people again?"

"O Sovereign Lord," I replied, "you alone know the
answer to that."

Then he said to me, "Speak a prophetic message to
these bones and say, 'Dry bones, listen to the word of the
Lord! This is what the Sovereign Lord says: Look! I am
going to put breath into you and make you live again! I will
put flesh and muscles on you and cover you with skin. I will
put breath into you, and you will come to life. Then you
will know that I am the Lord.'" (Ezekiel 37:1-6, NLT)

It's bizarre imagery until you consider the context of the passage.
When the Israelites had been exiled to Babylon because of their un-
faithfulness to God, they had lost their hope, their faith, and their
dreams for a future kingdom. Those dreams, along with all their
promises of *shalom* ("peace and prosperity"), had died, drying up like
old, decaying bones. They could see no hope, no way out. Yet God
was telling Ezekiel's generation that no matter how severe the loss,
no matter how far they had wandered away from his truth, no matter
how dry their faith had become or how hopeless their situation, he
would breathe new life into each new era of believers. He could do
this then, and he can do it now—regardless of the current popular
culture, economic state, or educational environment we may find
ourselves struggling to survive in. Good news indeed!

My hope is for you as parents to see that God can handle these unbelievable generational changes. They didn't catch him off guard. He is more than able to help us grow, endure, and overcome our parenting stresses and complications. He promises again and again in the Bible that he will show up. He is not going to leave us unprepared or unable to lead our kids into the path of life. Just as God led the children of Israel through the life and words of Ezekiel, God will provide direction and clarity in our lives when we stop long enough to listen. The path of life that he promises to us is the same one we need to lead our kids to follow. They will arrive safely, not because of our great wisdom or spiritual maturity, but because of our brokenness and humility. The key is to tune out our own preferences and instead cling tightly to his. It's really not complicated stuff. All we have to do is trust him and rely on his specific instructions to each of us.

Dangerous Assumptions

Reading about those reanimated bones was a powerful image. I wanted this kind of resurrection for my daughter. Our family crisis had brought me to a new understanding of God's grace and love, and I wanted to see Bethany—as well as Jessica and Caleb—understand these truths and be drawn into a vibrant relationship with God. I knew that was the real path to healing. But how could I get Bethany there? This wasn't something I could enforce through discipline. I had always been focused on the external. How could I encourage internal change?

In the past, I had been very aware of Bethany's behaviors, but not the condition of her heart. Although I was watching for her to comply outwardly with our rules and wishes, I was ignoring her inner feelings, beliefs, and emerging values under the surface of her compliance. I had put my energy into parental discipline and consistent rules enforcement, essentially using my parents' old strategy for raising me without any thought as to my goal. That was stupid, because their approach had totally failed for me—I'd reached adulthood as a Christian in name only. Why would I now expect the same approach to work for my daughter?

The truth is, I wasn't thinking at all. I was going through the parenting motions, mainly concerned with my own world and only casually noticing hers. I had become distracted and overly focused on my ministry duties and my own needs and wants. I was doing what I had been taught to do. In my mind, this was a formula to follow: Do the right stuff consistently, and your kids will eventually "get it" and become the wonderful Christian offspring we'd always imagined and hoped they would be. It sounds ridiculous, but that's what I really believed.

The reality, according to current research, is that more than half of all kids born into Christian families are walking away from the church. Rainer Research estimates that 70 percent of our youth abandon the church between the ages of eighteen and twenty-two.[2] In a climate like this, doing what we've always done just isn't going to work.

To successfully engage this generation of kids with the transformational truth of the gospel, we are going to have to be incredibly intentional. The passive, minimal-effort parenting approach I was using didn't work for my family, and it's not going to work any better for yours.

Somewhere in the past two decades, fathers' parenting styles became more passive, and the church in general did as well. Many leaders began to believe that if we could just entertain our kids as well as mainstream media did, then we could compete with these secular influences head-to-head and win our kids' hearts to Jesus. So the creation of "hip" church services was birthed, and the immediate response was terrific.

Unfortunately it didn't last very long. The mistake was compounded even more by parents who believed that if they just got their kids to these "hip" churches, they would somehow absorb the incredibly well-produced sermons, video presentations, and dramas, and all the essential values and beliefs of Christianity would become theirs for life. Absurd, right? But deep down that's what we and many of our counterparts believed—because it's what the majority of us who attend a modern fellowship of believers still continue to do. We're content to come to church once a week, toe the line behaviorally, and outwardly look like ideal Christians. God wants so much more for us, but too often we ignore it and stay with the safe, the tried-and-true: just enough God to make us feel good about our faith, but not enough to transform us from the inside out.

My friend Brian Hardin wrote this in his book *Passages*:

> When God decided to invade earth on the largest search and rescue mission in history, it was to redeem his people. We are those people, and yet our experience with God is too often limited to the sinner's prayer, Sunday service, occasional communion, and a higher moral code. Do we really believe that's all that God had in mind?[3]

Behavior Modification or Transformation?

Jesus addressed this issue over the course of his entire gospel ministry—the problem each generation has with seeking behavior modification instead of transformation. The brutal truth is this: Without God winning the battle in our hearts, we cannot be changed or transformed. The Pharisees, scribes, and Sadducees fought tenaciously with Jesus over the rules and politics of his time; they engaged in intellectual dogfights over their theological beliefs and opinions. They were proud, educated men who knew every phrase of the Scriptures by memory but resisted the message of the heart that Jesus kept preaching to them in one parable after another. In the end, they so resented what he was saying that they killed him.

The battle between the mind and the heart rages on. The mind wants to understand God, to grasp the nature of our salvation, to comprehend the significance of grace and of new life. It's far too busy trying to *understand* the love of God to actually *experience* it. The mind wants to control its surroundings, to subdue all possible threats or undesired outcomes before they occur, to avoid risk and anything uncomfortable, to be entertained and engaged and flattered and loved and pleasured. When we put the mind first, we seek to find significance in ourselves, to use God and faith as excuses for pursuing our own ambitions. We discipline ourselves so we can enjoy the pride of personal accomplishment and the adoration of those who can't do what we can. This is the mind-set of our human nature, and as parents we will always drift this way if we are left to our own devices.

Knowing how we think, God speaks directly to our hearts. He is aware that if we seek to follow after him with just our heads, we will fail. We'll end up reducing faith to a list of rules instead of a living, breathing relationship. We'll know about God without really knowing him. The gift of life and grace comes out of our acceptance of God's love—first in our hearts, and then in our minds. This had been my personal faith struggle. After what happened to Bethany, God helped me to unlearn what I thought I knew about him, my faith, and the ways he works in our lives. I had a partial intellectual grasp of the life he promised, but not a clear view of how to share it with my family. My heart needed to catch up with my mind before

I would be in any position to effectively lead my family spiritually. I was learning on the job, and by God's infinite patience and grace with me, it still wasn't too late.

When parenting or discipleship focuses primarily on the head—the external issues of behavior and verbal compliance—we may be in serious danger of missing the entire point. Jesus focused his teachings and energy on reaching our hearts, not on the externals. He taught this principle in the Sermon on the Mount and in parables to his disciples. He preached this same basic lesson for three years, over and over again, like he was worried we might forget it. The repetition of this message proves its significance. In almost every sermon we find in the Gospels, Jesus is teaching us to listen with our hearts, to love wholeheartedly, or to respond to the Kingdom message at a heart level.

Let's take some words from the prophet Isaiah as an example:

The Spirit of the Sovereign LORD is upon me, for the LORD has anointed me to bring good news to the poor. He has sent me to comfort the brokenhearted and to proclaim that captives will be released and prisoners will be freed. (Isaiah 61:1, NLT)

The Gospels record that Jesus himself quoted this passage, bridging this theme of both the Old and New Testaments for us to consider. His message is not just to save us from hell or to keep us from making the same mistakes that our parents made. No, his purpose is to address the condition of our hearts. To comfort the brokenhearted and bring hope to those who have none. To set the captives free! As parents, we should share the same focus for our kids. What about their hearts?

If the Bible seems to prioritize this issue, it must be important. It must also be critical advice for us as parents in our struggle to raise kids who genuinely want to follow in the footsteps of Jesus.

So how do we help our kids hear with their hearts and not just their heads? Do we develop a better curriculum with more heart topics, filled with more emotional metaphors of God's love for them? Do we pull back from teaching them about the Scriptures and the need for self-control and purity, in an effort to gain their trust and win their hearts? No!

I'm convinced that reaching our youth is not about rejecting past approaches or throwing out the stricter applications of parenting discipline. Instead, I believe it's about implementing those beliefs and traditions with a greater understanding of the *goal* of Christian parenting: *to lead our own children to a lifelong and intimate relationship with the one who made them and loves them more than we could ever comprehend.*

How do we reach that goal? I think it's all about connecting—being present for our children, being real with them, and getting to know them on a deeper level.

Without actions, our words are merely ideas that sometimes, maybe, kind of penetrate our kids' hearts . . . for about 3.5 seconds. Then they evaporate into the atmosphere, never to return. But actions? Those stick. When we take the time to interact with our kids, without making every discussion a serious learning moment or a life lesson, we are starting the process of connecting. Our actions of love and sacrifice become the catalyst for reaching their hearts, not just their minds. We have to help them connect the love and hope and peace that we claim is in Jesus with the real-life, here-and-now world of our homes. It's a critical first step in building a credible foundation for their faith.

Critical Factors to Connecting

The first and most important ingredient to connecting with our kids is time. When we skip time with our kids for something else, we had better be sure it's something God is leading us to do, not a matter of convenience or preference on our part. The ultimate and universal language of love is *time*. No shortcuts, no faking it. Your kids will know, and they will understand that when it comes to being a parent, your heart just isn't in it. If you approach parenting like you do work or hobbies or friendships, you will have a much harder time with this. Parenting is the biggest thing in our lives beside our covenant with God and our spouses. It is our solemn responsibility to guide our kids in the ways of life. We cannot do that effectively from a distance.

When our kids grow up a little bit and don't need constant supervision, it's easy to let go of that tight connection. But it may be that tweens and teens are at the most essential ages for needing parental involvement. George Barna writes,

> During the 11 to 13 age range, most kids undergo huge changes and challenges related to their self-image and their choices concerning morals, beliefs, relationships, and life goals. It often becomes a difficult time in the relationship between parents and kids, but it is also one of the most critical times for parents to make sure they stay connected and accessible to their kids.[4]

When we spend time with our kids, we are speaking love to them in a very tangible way. Time invested in our children conveys, in a thousand different ways, our desire to be with them, our acceptance of them as they are, the treasure we consider them to be, their tremendous value and purpose. It validates their unique identity and immeasurable worth—things they must have securely in their hearts to safely transition from the turbulent teen years and become healthy adults.

For many parents, the challenge is this: Will we agree to take the time and energy needed to be with our family? To step back from the urgency of our life plans and sacrifice of ourselves to know our children's specific needs? If you've been through a crisis, it will take your fullest effort and dedication to gain your children's trust again, and it will most likely not come from doing things you would choose to do for fun on your own. So while you're suffering through your second hour of *SpongeBob SquarePants* or are lost in some insane video racing game on Xbox 360, the activity itself won't matter because you will suddenly be so aware of the amazing child you call your own. It will become a genuinely beautiful time you share together.

If you're a parent of girls, be prepared to drive to Sonic or Dairy Queen for ice cream and know that you will sit for several awkward minutes before your teen daughter starts to share with you about the things that matter most to her. It may take some serious mall time looking at girlie trinkets and five-dollar jewelry kiosks, but it's worth every investment to prove to your kids that you are interested in them, that you are intentionally engaged in knowing them, and that they mean more to you than your golf handicap or the play-by-play broadcasts of your favorite sports team.

Authenticity of living is the second critical component to connecting with our kids in any age or culture. If we have any hope of gaining the respect and trust of our children, our words and actions must be compatible. That's absolutely nonnegotiable when it comes to passing our faith on to our kids.

Our lives are full of people and causes that make sweeping motivational promises, but in fact, fail to deliver. Our world is the ultimate tease, and when our young teens start to pay attention to the messages they hear, they will quickly sense when someone is being disingenuous. They are sick to death of the failed promises we make, of the slick infomercials and the showy marketing of the gospel. The last thing they can tolerate is seeing that the values we as their parents are forcing them to respect are undermined by our daily choices.

Being authentic isn't about living a perfectly consistent or balanced life. The fact is, we're not always healthy and balanced and poised and calm. We're all struggling and growing in our faith. We're weak and broken people, beaten down by life more often than we care to admit. No, living authentically with our kids isn't about being perfect. It's about the need for us to own up to our shortcomings with them. To be authentic, we must admit when we blow it, when our kids notice an inconsistency in our behavior and call us out on it. They will usually do this in a less-than-gentle manner, and the temptation will be to nail them for disrespect and rebellion. But if you consider their rebuke carefully in your heart, you may realize that, regardless of their personal motivations in the matter, they could be right.

It is critical that we recognize our kids' need for authentic role models and allow them to see us as the flawed human beings we are. We must strive to be parents who have learned to live firmly grounded in the grip of our Savior's grace. We can't try vainly to convince our children that if they become Christians, life will be fun and happy all the time, without the tribulation and stress of normal life. So many of us try to live out our Christianity as superficially holy, "keeping it all together," pseudo-disciples of a plastic faith, never touched publicly or privately by the impact of sin or fear or depression. We tuck all our problems inside and hide them—until our kids find them and push them back in our faces. If they don't verbalize this, you might think

you've gotten away with it, that they haven't noticed the gap between
your rules and your behavior. Don't kid yourself. They might not call
your bluff to your face, but believe me, they see it. They know the
reality; they will find the Wizard of Oz hidden behind the curtain.

As C. S. Lewis writes in *Mere Christianity*,

> A Christian society is not going to arrive until most of us
> really want it: and we are not going to want it until we
> become fully Christian. I may repeat "Do as you would be
> done by" till I am black in the face, but I cannot really carry
> it out till I love my neighbor as myself: and I cannot learn
> to love my neighbor as myself till I learn to love God: and
> I cannot learn to love God except by learning to obey Him.
> And so, as I warned you, we are driven on to something more
> inward—driven on from social matters to religious matters.[5]

Let's agree to drop the veil of religiosity and accept that our teens
need to see us in the down and dirty moments of our real-life days.
We must choose as flawed parents to live with grace for each other
and be ready to share that grace with our kids when they blow it.
This is *essential* if we hope they will ever extend grace back to us when
we fall short. The power of authentic living as a parent is all about
apologizing the minute we overreact or make inaccurate assumptions
about our children's actions or attitudes. It's about living in humility
and grace and truth. If our Christianity is real, it's got to be deep and
thick, covering every aspect of our lives. Our faith must be present in
our marriages, our work, and our friendships. Our love must endure
there, in the messiness of life, if we are to gain any chance at earning
our children's genuine trust and respect—and ultimately handing
down our faith to the next generation.

When Connection Falls Short

When we compartmentalize our faith and shortchange our kids with our time, energy, and focus, we are creating an environment where they will retreat from us. Instead of growing closer to us, they will back away and ultimately shut their hearts to our words—because our lives fail to demonstrate the reality we claim they need to be happy, satisfied, or "saved." The tragedy for many families comes when our kids start to confuse us, their inconsistent parents, as being similar in nature to God. If we allow that to happen, we have effectively made them cynics of the goodness and reliable character of God himself, and in time, they likely will reject the important truths and values we are so desperate to teach them. They won't usually throw a fit or articulate what they are sensing in our unauthentic lifestyles, but as they grow up, they will simply begin to look elsewhere for an explanation of their existence and purpose in life.

Our kids look to us for unconditional love and acceptance. However, as Christian parents we sometimes have a hard time accepting them as they are because we so desperately want them to become something else: professing Christians. It's too easy to try to validate ourselves by our kids. And for parents who are in ministry or Christian leadership, the pressure to make our kids shining examples of spiritual role models is especially huge. Yet if we take a genuine love for who they are and turn it into a mechanical and somewhat selfish desire for them to just accept Christ because that will make us look good, we're sending the wrong message. We're telling them that their value rests only in their agreement with us. Aside from alienating our children, the deeper danger is that they might temporarily respond to the gospel just to gain our approval.

The problem is, when our kids profess their faith only to win our favor, their relationship with Jesus gains no significant reality. Then their spirituality comes out mostly as learned, theological terms, combined with memorization of key Scriptures to quote when appropriate. They may follow along dutifully in a desperate attempt to gain our attention and win our love, and it may look good for a while. But when they hit the high school and college years, we'll have kids whose spirituality is empty—nothing but a shallow declaration of faith after a brief summer church camp or a "repeat after me" sinner's prayer. Jesus and Christianity just won't stick when the challenges of choices and freedom and independence come, and I believe that's because this type of faith wasn't ever settled in their hearts. It was just a shadow, a copy of the genuine thing. It didn't transform our kids from the inside out; it compressed them from the outside in. I'm afraid our homes and churches are full of such double-minded youth, just waiting to escape the confines of the superficial and leave our sheltered homes, schools, and churches behind. Because we weren't authentic in our faith, they have become completely uninterested in what Christians claim to be.

Our aim as parents is often to justify ourselves to our peers and confirm to the world what a great family we turned out to be. Yet our children slowly simmer in their resentment and frustration at being little more than a public display of pride for their parents, a trophy for other, more dysfunctional families to envy and admire.

They sense in our urgent schedules that we're just barely keeping up with life. In our repeated outbreaks of anxiety and fear at their choices, we're really displaying to our kids that we're not very stable ourselves. They start to disrespect us when they notice that our Sunday affirmations of being in a good place with God don't match our Monday morning panic attacks. They will use those inconsistencies to conveniently skip their own personal contemplation of God and faith, chalking it all up as a big charade that their parents are hung up on. After all, that's what the vast majority of our world tells them about Christians: we're just a bunch of religion-obsessed hypocrites with double standards, eager to judge others while parading our false virtue.

A Divine Strategy Emerges

We see the dangers, and we don't want to fall into those traps. So how can we find the right kind of time to spend with our kids? How can we grow in authenticity? How can we connect so deeply with our children that they will be open to God's working in their lives? Is it even possible to get from here to there? How can we make up for the lack of spiritual reality in our homes?

We have to remember the message of the story about the dry bones. God is in the business of resurrection. Just as he resurrected the dry bones as Ezekiel watched, he is able to do miraculous works in your family. He can bring new life to a faith that once seemed dead and renewed love to a household that once was full of discord. And what's more, he has promised to continue working in our lives and our kids' lives. Philippians 1:6 says, "I am certain that God, who began the good work within you, will continue his work until it is finally finished on the day when Christ Jesus returns" (NLT). He has a plan for your family. Trust him.

The foundation of everything is listening to God. It's so critical that we learn how to be still long enough to consistently hear God, asking him for help regularly, accepting his advice, and watching for his real solutions to whatever problems we're facing at home.

As you seek God's direction, I believe you will receive a special insight for each child and each situation you encounter. You will find God both in the little issues and in the huge, life-changing crisis that wakes you in the night, like mine did. God will slowly reveal to you the particular weaknesses and strengths of your kids, and he will equip you with the knowledge you need to pray for them effectively and specifically. As redemption flows into their lives, you'll be amazed at how their issues are resolved and their burdens released.

Whatever God reveals to you as a parent, the solution will connect your hearts together as a family. It will awaken your inner being and activate the one thing that makes you most passionate, most creative, and most alive. God's plan for your family will *not* deaden your senses or cause you to snore; it will be electric in its attraction and impact. Rest assured, it won't be a one-size-fits-all plan. Not at all! God's solution will show up at just the perfect time and in just the perfect way, custom-fitted to work just for you!

For our family, the larger solution came through a summer road trip to America's Wild West and the rugged beauty of the Canadian frontier. It stretched us beyond our comfort zones and required a tremendous sacrifice of time and energy, but it was the precise prescription we needed for our family's health, healing, and transformation of faith. God inspired us to strike out in a new direction—to do something big, something out of the ordinary that allowed us for a short period to put family togetherness at the very top of our priority list and find new ways to connect and interact.

The trip changed our lives and won our hearts. But it was not born out of my deep intellectual insight or from the wise counsel of a leader in my life. It came from time spent on my knees before God and from the glimmer of an idea deep in my heart. I had a passion I had longed to share with my kids but just didn't know how, and God showed me the way. It will be the same for you if you genuinely seek from God a way to recover the losses in your own family and life. A way to offset the insidious and powerful dark forces that rob you of your hope and joy and passion for living. God will provide a time for your faith to be renewed, for you to understand his grace anew and to let that be your motivation for everything. A time for you to learn to be authentic with your kids. A time for you to allow them to see how real God is, how he is working in your soul and theirs. It will be beautiful to see and feel, and you will probably be surprised by how God will choose to work.

If you seek him honestly and humbly, God will use the passions in your own life to reconnect you with your family and bring your relationships into a healthier place, with more authenticity than ever before. It will take time. This transformation will not happen overnight, and it may require you to be uncomfortable. But in the end you'll be following God's custom-designed solution. And I believe you'll find that if you trust him with the journey, the destination will take care of itself.

This parenting adventure we have with God is the most powerful and fulfilling thing we have ever been invited to experience, and if it's genuine, the results last forever. God wants to win your heart and your kids' hearts. Nothing less will do; nothing less will work. When we're all out of answers and strategies, when we feel our society is disintegrating around us, it's time to stop repeating our past mistakes. We have to be simple and sincere. We need to actively pursue knowing the mind of God and seeking his wisdom in our parenting decisions. Ask God to give you the courage and strength to embark afresh on your own path, your personal pilgrimage from surviving parenthood to thriving in it. Learn to embrace the road ahead, and gain enough perspective along the way to take the time to enjoy the view. Step back from living life as a safe and predictable commute and understand that God's path will be an unpredictable one. It's not easy and it's not heavily trafficked, but in the end, when you reach the mountaintop, the extraordinary view is worth all the effort to get there.

It's time to get real, time to trust God with our hearts and the
hearts of our children. Let's allow ourselves to discover his solution,
to follow his road map to recovery and reconnection with our kids. I
believe that as you ask God for this renewal, it is already on its way.
Look for it. Wait for it. Trust in it. Go for it. No other plan will do.

> Now to him who is able to keep you from stumbling and to
> present you blameless before the presence of his glory with
> great joy, to the only God, our Savior, through Jesus Christ
> our Lord, be glory, majesty, dominion, and authority, before
> all time and now and forever. Amen. (Jude 1:24-25, ESV)

Consider these words of encouragement from writer and pastor
Pete Greig:

> With blood and sweat and many tears, with sleepless nights
> and fruitless days, they pray as if it all depends on God and
> live as if it all depends on them.
> Their DNA chooses JESUS. (He breathes out, they
> breathe in.) Their subconscious sings. They had a blood
> transfusion with Jesus. . . .
> They walk tall and trees applaud, skyscrapers bow,
> mountains are dwarfed by these children of another
> dimension. Their prayers summon the hounds of heaven
> and invoke the ancient dream of Eden.
> And this vision will be.
> It will come to pass; it will come easily; it will come soon.
> How do I know?
> Because this is the longing of creation itself, the groaning
> of the Spirit, the very dream of God.

My tomorrow is his today. My distant hope is his 3D.
And my feeble, whispered, faithless prayer invokes a
thunderous, resounding, bone-shaking great "Amen!" from
countless angels, from heroes of the faith, from Christ
himself. And he is the original dreamer, the ultimate winner.
Guaranteed.

PETE GREIG, *THE VISION AND THE VOW*[6]

PART II
On the Road

FIVE

MY FAMILY ON A ROAD TRIP: GENIUS OR INSANITY?

The most extraordinary thing in the world is an ordinary man and an ordinary woman and their ordinary children.   G. K. CHESTERTON

As I REFLECTED on all our family had been through in the past months and as I spent time with God in prayer, asking him for guidance, I sensed that God's specific strategy to help us reconnect as a family included taking a road trip out west.

Despite all my previous rhetoric about letting God lead us on our road to recovery, I wasn't thrilled with his plan. A family road trip? For all of us, at one time? This idea, while at first supercool and attractive to my explorer's heart, became less exciting after a few moments of sane contemplation.

Five people in one vehicle for at least a week or maybe longer. Two teenage girls and one seventh-grade son all together with my wife and me in a box on wheels, a steel cage not much bigger than a king-size bed. Hmmm. This could create some serious tension after only thirty minutes on the road!

My previous driving experiences with the five of us being in one consolidated space for any length of time were not good. So far, most trips had ended up with one or more of the kids getting seriously ticked off and causing a huge uproar. Sometimes they even dragged my wife or me into the fray. It was always loud, and it was always unpleasant.

I had learned to accept such relational traveling dangers some time ago. But this was different. Our previous adventures had been simple, three-and-a-half-hour trips to Memphis and back where we visited with Paige's family. What would an extended, multi-state, seven-thousand-mile road trip do to our family and my sanity? It seemed like a pretty bad idea to me. *Really, God?* I found myself asking. *Your best solution for our very messed-up and often irritable family is to cram us all into an SUV for two weeks and let us duke it out?* I was not impressed.

The Family Dynamic

To this point in our story, I've been talking mainly about our middle child, Bethany Rose. But of course we do have two other kids, Jessica Elaine and Caleb Andrew. As with all children, ours have their unique strengths and weaknesses. They exhibit varying behavior patterns, conflicting personalities, social preferences, and unusual little quirks. These multiple siblings and differing personalities can create negative intrafamily competitions, and those can make for some very challenging parenting issues. I've discovered that regardless of your own personality, you are virtually guaranteed that one or more of your kids will have a completely opposite style of communication, usually with lots of antagonistic interests, bizarre tastes, and annoying personal habits that will remind you of your spouse! Our daughters, for example, remain polar opposites and are like oil and water. They do not easily mix.

As you read on, I hope you will be able to identify with the various personality types in our family. Maybe some of our kids' characteristics are represented in your own home. No two children are exactly alike, but some family dynamics are common to every home regardless of socioeconomic background or ethnic identity. Our story will most certainly overlap with your own. Our hope is that it will provide you with some comfort and encouragement that you, too, can reconnect with your children, and in the process, pass your faith on to them in the years to come.

Jessica

Jessica is our oldest. At the time of this story she was sixteen, fresh out of her sophomore year of high school. Learning to drive a car, she was experiencing freedom and independence in a greater way than ever before. Not that she needed any prodding to mature or become more independent. Her personality is that of a typical firstborn. A leader in the home, she is eager to direct the younger kids to fall in line with whatever the family is doing. She is unafraid to share her opinions with others and sees the world in a black-and-white kind of way. We teasingly call her the "literalist," as she often ponders casual statements for their actual meaning when others understand them as off-the-cuff remarks. Her childhood tendency to obey first and ask questions later (or never) made her an ideal kid to parent. Compliant and respectful, she exhibited all the great stereotypes of a "perfect" little girl. She was the envy of our parenting peers and the favorite student of most of her teachers.

To this day, Jessica continues to earn straight-A honors every grading period. Others know her as a diligent student and avid learner. Jessica loves books and libraries and avoids malls, shopping, and makeup. She loves to curl up in her room and read or watch movies all day. She has few friends, but the ones she has are strong and enduring. She is fascinated by foreign cultures, languages, and ideas; she loves art, literature, and classic films. Jessica is a smart, articulate, and responsible young woman, and she creates a very long shadow for Bethany to live under.

Being so responsible and a firstborn, Jessica is most comfortable when she can control her environment. For instance, she hates to attend social events where she knows few people or when she has little interest in the event's purpose. She attended one dance at her high school and swore never again—not because she couldn't find a date, but because she hated the "pointlessness" of it. Jessica is not comfortable speaking in public but will freely share her mind to those she lives with or is around for any length of time.

Jessica saves money like a miser, carefully considering before buying anything. She was a babysitter in high demand for our neighbors and made a good side income that allowed her to save up enough money to buy her first car at age sixteen. She doesn't crave anything but dark chocolate, good books, and antique garage sales. She carefully avoids the frenzy of teen style and drama whenever possible and defers to more subtle and mature clothing, activities, and interests. Jessica remains a decade ahead of most teens emotionally and mentally, and she longs to be in college, far away from the insecurities and inconsistencies of high school. Careful, deliberate, and thoughtful, she is wise beyond her years and eager to get on with the business of adulthood.

Jessica's spirituality began at an early age, and her earnest interest in Sunday school, Jesus, and the Bible was evident from the beginning. Her teen and adolescent encounters with fake or hypocritical youth group kids did jade her significantly, but overall she was able to embrace her faith as her own. From a young age until adulthood, her faith continued to grow and expand from a personal salvation experience to a desire to help and serve others.

Jessica viewed her sister as "unreachable" after several years of repeated disagreements, offenses, and isolation. By the time Bethany reached eighth grade and Jessica was in her freshman year of high school, most of the time they retreated to their respective bedrooms just to avoid each other. Jessica had decided to leave her sister to her own devices, and that was just fine with Bethany. They had a deep rift between them—not something Jessica wanted, but she had grown to accept it as reality and something she couldn't change on her own. As a result, Jessica had developed a rather nasty condescension toward her younger sister, something that Bethany strongly disliked and reacted to.

In the end, the girls developed an insolent tolerance for each other. In our presence they avoided most disagreements, but they both harbored sullen resentment toward each other. Our home life suffered noticeably. Bethany pulled further and further away from her sister, while we as her naive parents blindly assumed that their fights, although frequent, were nothing more than the normal sibling rivalry of hormonal teen girls. Jessica warned us it went deeper than that, but at the time we couldn't see it.

Bethany

From reading our story so far, you already have a good idea of Bethany's personality. As a child, she often seemed to exhibit the challenges and traits of the stereotypical second child. As the self-titled "black sheep" of our family, she always seems to pick a harder way to do things than her sister and brother do. With an older sister like Jessica just fourteen months ahead of her, Bethany always felt as though she were inferior or less valuable to Paige and me. Incredibly sensitive to any form of injustice or favoritism, she was the child who began many sentences with the classic "It's not fair . . ." and ended them with a *humph* of frustration when she didn't get her way.

Given the contrast between her sister's compliance and Bethany's resistance to any form of authority or discipline, it is easy to see how their sibling dynamic quickly eroded from early childhood playmates to adolescent rivals. Jessica would go out of her way to remind Bethany of her seniority in age and grade, and Bethany would go out of her way to show Jessica how much she didn't care. Riding in a car with them in the backseat was asking for trouble. Sparks were going to fly. How much and how hot it got would depend only on the length of the trip.

Bethany is fascinated by external things like money, appearance, social standing, and boys. The complete opposite of her sister, she loves to spend an entire day at the local mall and cruise through the various shops and eateries with some cash in one hand and a cell phone in the other. She loves to buy things—shoes, blouses, jewelry, makeup, jeans, you name it. If it glitters or sparkles in the light, she has to have it. If there happens to be a dollar in her pocket, she will spend it.

Full of vibrant energy and passion, Bethany has a short fuse and a bright smile. She can rise and fall from depression to ecstatic joy and from confidence to frustration in mere seconds. Her educational experiences are similar to her sister's, but with less interest in learning and more in achieving. Bethany sees school as a chance to interact with her peers and hang out with her friends. She makes straight As too, but she seems to focus far less on the homework and more on the approval of her teachers. If she thinks a teacher is terrible, she candidly expresses it to anyone who will listen. Bethany has been to several high school dances and enjoys dressing up immensely. She considers fashion and pop culture to be incredibly cool and stays as relevant and modern as possible in her appearance and actions.

She speaks like a machine gun, fast and furiously. Her words come out in brisk torrents. She has been accused of being "snotty" and of "not taking crap from anyone." This is true. Several young men have tried to date her, but none have succeeded for long. She is intense and focused, her attention moving quickly from one idea or activity to another. She craves action and despises sitting still or being alone. Bethany is moody, often going through significant transitions of attitude, behavior, and appearance from day to day. Frequently defiant, she often tried to sneak around us to do things she knew we would not approve of—leaving her older sister to "rat her out" from time to time.

At the time of this story, Bethany's spiritual status was vague and undefined. She had rejected almost everything we had tried to encourage her to do, more as a basic assertion of her identity and independence than of her actual resistance to what we believed. Regardless of her motivations, she had failed to embrace the Christian faith personally at all. She was hostile to any suggestion that she could pray about something that was bothering her. She didn't use her Bible or pay any attention to church or youth group, and she didn't pretend otherwise. She was openly skeptical of faith, God, and Christians in general, and she greatly resented the legalistic nature of many who tried to impose their beliefs on her.

As a young woman, she was confident in her ability to find her own happiness and success in life without depending on her parents, other people, or God. To Bethany, finding her elusive Prince

Charming was all that mattered. She believed with all her heart that there was a fine young man out there who would sweep her off her feet and rescue her from her boring and rigid family, and she was determined to be ready for him when he appeared. Nicholas Sparks's films were her favorite, and she lived firmly in the grip of the romantic fantasy that love would satisfy all her wants and needs.

God did not fit into her life equation beyond being a distant possibility for her to consider someday. She was unwilling to wait for much in her life, especially something as vital to her as a boyfriend, and God's rules were too restrictive for her taste. She wanted to experience life and to discover for herself if the values we espoused were actually her own. She had never really liked anyone to help her at any time in her young life, and asking God to do so was not an option. She ignored our concerns and refused to listen to our advice.

Bethany now says that when she reached rock bottom, she had been praying and asking God for help. But in her mind, God had abandoned her to be molested—and then rejected by her family. She was out of answers and too frustrated with God to recognize his voice of love and grace in her life. She became frantic to find acceptance, to feel love and loyalty from her friends since she had given up on finding that in her own home. It was a tragic way to live, but on the outside she was quite capable of putting on every appearance that she was in charge, doing well, and above needing anyone's support. She was the master of disguising her true emotions, and as her family, we had grown so weary of her anger and irritations that we quit trying to understand what was really going on inside her heart.

Caleb

Our son, Caleb, is a survivor. He has, after all, endured more than a decade of growing up with two older sisters nagging at him—not an easy thing to do. At the time of the trip, he had just finished the seventh grade and had hated every day of it. Junior high has to be the worst time for kids in general. The pace of education and the stress of social development, combined with the physical changes of adolescence, are not fun. New emotions, powerful hormones, basic immaturity, overall weirdness, embarrassing pimples, and shorter boys alongside taller, more developed girls all make for a mishmash of nothing but awkwardness. No exceptions, no escape . . . junior high was and is a bummer.

Caleb was smack-dab in the middle of all that during this entire narrative, and true to his personality, he stayed in the shadows most of the time. Caleb is a thinker. He's smarter than his sisters intellectually but way behind them socially. Caleb prefers to stay home whenever possible. He is *not* a traveler of any sort. He hates to take trips or drives, and good luck convincing him to come along on an errand. Nothing is more repulsive to him than that.

Caleb loves technology. First it was Game Boy, then Wii, and now PlayStation 3. Electronics are his closest companions. He loves to listen to music on his iPod whenever he is not at school or asleep. Caleb is a quiet and calculating young man, soft-spoken and funny as can be. His humor and wit are legendary in our home, as he often shares his observations about his teachers, fellow students, or his sisters with such accuracy and sarcasm that he could be a stand-up comic. Caleb is not an athletic guy; he prefers the keyboard or piano and enjoys soaking in the richness of music and the world of modern alternative rock.

Being around the music and media hub of Nashville, Caleb has been exposed to numerous indie Christian rock and pop bands over the years and has absorbed their influences deeply. He has a sharp and well-tuned ear for emerging new bands and artists, and he keeps a huge library of music files on his multiple iPods. Unconcerned with girls or fashion or social popularity, Caleb exhibits a quiet kind of cool that seems to impress others. He fights with his sisters as much as any other brother does, but usually his survival instincts take over and he flees the scene as quickly as possible. He hates confrontation in general and always seeks to avoid further exasperation from his sisters' heavy-handed ways and dominating personalities.

As the youngest, Caleb has been spoiled the most by Paige and me. He always got extra gifts at Christmas, on his birthday, and from his grandparents. In many ways, he benefited from our desire to delay his maturation as long as possible. Knowing he would be our last child, we were happy to let him grow up slowly. As the "baby" in the house, he was often treated with extra-special sensitivity and compassion. He is also a procrastinator. He carefully avoids work whenever possible, preferring mental challenges to physical ones. Caleb can live happily in a dirty, disheveled room for weeks on end and not feel any need to clean it until someone forces him to. In that regard, he's a normal teen.

Caleb can also be silly. He loves to harass and tease his sisters by dancing, farting, spitting, and twisting around with the oddest noises and sounds he can create from whatever body part seems to be working at the time. They both hate it. He loves to see them hate it. They annoy each other in all combinations. Caleb and Bethany in a car are impossible for the fighting; Caleb and Jessica in a car are ridiculously silly. As parents, we have to pick our poison, so to speak. We separate them as their moods require whenever we travel.

At the time of this story, Caleb's spirituality was similar to that of most preteen boys—casually interested in God based on his circumstances. When at church or Sunday school he listened and occasionally interacted, but mostly he remained passive to the message of the day. When at school or home he had little interest in God, didn't read his Bible, and didn't show the slightest interest in our infrequent family devotions. He was respectful, quiet, and compliant, but he was content to live without any real challenges to his thinking or behavior.

He wasn't angry or bitter toward God, but he wasn't sensing any real need to have God in his day-to-day life either. He had prayed a sinner's prayer at an FFH (Far From Home) concert several years earlier and had acted the part of a good Christian by behaving at school, staying out of trouble, and avoiding porn and drugs. He was really a model child in every respect outwardly, but inwardly he avoided anything remotely spiritual whenever he could.

Caleb hates to ride long distances. Our annual migration to Raleigh, North Carolina, to see my brother's family was about the longest he had ever allowed himself to be stuck in a vehicle. He abhorred long stretches of sharing space with his sisters. He either drove them nuts with his annoying habits and false voices, or they enraged him with their personal space needs and intolerance of his bodily functions. Traveling with Caleb and his sisters was like living out a scene from a National Lampoon's Vacation film—slightly inappropriate, disrespectful, embarrassing, and insane, but for brief moments . . . bordering on ridiculously funny.

Paige

I love my wife. She is a treasure and all that I am not. She is the most amazing woman I have ever known, besides my mother. Though she is a full foot shorter and two years older than I am (something I love to remind her of), she seems at times to be decades wiser. Full of patience and concern, she is careful, considerate, and slow to react in most situations. She often enjoys observing more than actively participating. After more than twenty years together, I can honestly say that Paige exemplifies the biblical standard of a Proverbs 31 woman. She is beautiful inside and out, hardworking, careful, and attentive to her family and home. She is a public school teacher with a genuine desire to help kids learn and grow. Focused on ESL (English as a second language) classrooms, she works primarily with Hispanic elementary students.

She loves her home. When Paige arrives home from work, she almost immediately changes into sweats and tennis shoes or takes a long, hot bath. She considers her house and family to be her retreat from the demands of her job. Her personality is "slow and steady," and she prefers things around her to be stable, predictable, and ordered. She does not like rapid transitions, unexpected changes, or rash decisions. She is trustworthy, faithful, and loyal to a fault. Like Jessica, she has few friends, but those she has last for life. She is considerate of her family and alert to their slightest annoyance or frustration. Paige is not a fan of adventures or spontaneous trips. I have tried on many occasions to get her to join me on my last-minute diversions, but she prefers to stay at home and enjoy her books or flowers or HGTV programs.

My wife will often go well out of her way to avoid any confrontation or disagreement, either at work or in our home. Paige and Jessica are very close and can communicate easily most of the time, and the same is true with Caleb. But she and Bethany have often butted heads and had some real challenges in connecting. Bethany's personality is so much the opposite of my wife's that it was a constant irritation for them to try to spend time together, shop together, or just be mom and daughter together. Their relationship was so strained that I often needed to step in to help resolve their growing conflicts from getting out of hand. My wife did the same for me with Jessica and to some degree with Caleb as he got older.

When we traveled or took long trips, I usually hung out with Bethany while Paige spent time with the other two. We tended to split them up in the seating of our minivan so we could divide and conquer on the way. This worked most of the time but not always. Paige would sometimes run out of even her extraordinary patience and blast into one of the kids for their immaturity or selfishness. Paige is a "like to get there" kind of vacationer, and I'm an "exploring is the journey" kind of guy. She wants to get to the resort and rest, while I'm unconcerned about arriving anywhere at any particular time, being much more interested in the scenery and adventure along the way.

Paige's spirituality is strong. Her faith had endured my marital infidelity years earlier and had strengthened her identity and independence in the shadow of my often overbearing personality and temperament. Although she has had bouts of depression and fatigue common to working mothers of three, she never suffered from seriously debilitating illness or despair. She has a great capacity for trusting God in her life but sometimes struggles with trusting him for her kids' lives. She tends to need more control and influence over their day-to-day activities than I do. In the case of Bethany after our crisis, it was a real challenge for Paige to let her daughter leave our home, go out in public, attend high school, and be vulnerable to danger.

For Paige, spontaneous faith and emotional inspiration are less important than having a strategy for coping with problems. I'm more comfortable letting God just show up and start to miraculously "do his thing." She wants to see tangible changes and budgets and timetables for solving issues. She is much tighter with finances than I am; she hates spending too much money for Christmas or birthdays or special trips. It was a challenge for me to get her even to consider spending the little money we had on a two-week road-trip vacation into the wilderness.

Brad

I'm a bit of a parenting mess. At six feet three inches and at least 240 pounds, I'm a big, awkward guy. My personality is driven, but I'm mellowing with age. I'm intense at work and passive at home. I've always been a leader, from the earliest I can recall until now. I live life at full speed, rarely if ever putting my foot on the brakes. I love to fix things in other people but hate to allow it to be done to me. I can be impetuous, stubborn, and arrogant. I often speak much more force-fully than I feel, and most people mistake my impatience for anger or condescension. I'm all about getting results and reaching goals. I hate to wait. I'm anxious to avoid being common or predictable, and I love to surprise others with gifts.

I can be as gregarious and outgoing as I can be introspective and isolated, depending on the situation and my mood. I love to explore new things, places, or ideas. I'm a natural optimist, able to oversim-plify a complex issue out of my desire for it to be easy, rather than my belief that it is. I have been known to exaggerate from time to time (although that seems to be fading in my forties) as I tell a story or share a point. I am passionate and full of confidence on the outside but often unsure and fearful inside.

My background has allowed me to live through a great many things, professionally and personally. I've worked as a manager for McDonald's, and I've been an active chiropractic physician. I've been involved with politics and our local homeowners association but have failed to make a single PTA meeting in my life. I love my kids. I would crawl over glass naked to save them if I had to. I love to hang out with my family, but I have to fight to find the time. I am concerned about the nature of media and its inordinate influence on our kids and their beliefs, and I devote much of my time to my job as the president of a Christian preteen media group in Nashville. I serve as a copastor in my local community and remain motivated to help provide kids with alternatives that are as entertaining as they are wholesome.

I'm a hard-core adventure junkie. I love to take drives into

unknown territory and explore foreign landscapes. I've driven almost
every major highway or two-lane road in Colorado over the past decade, usually with Brian Hardin, who remains my dearest friend and
comrade. I'm particularly drawn to high mountains and dense alpine
woods. Northern New Mexico, Colorado, Wyoming, and Montana
are some of my favorite places at any time of the year. In our travels,
I've logged well over 500,000 miles from Maine to Seattle and everywhere in between. Road trips are my way to escape, my retreat from
the tedium of a nine-to-five job and the pressures of public ministry
and a relentless work schedule. I find solace and refreshment in the
beauty of the wild and untamed lands we explore.

I have failed at my life in every conceivable way. I've experienced
the ruin of my marriage and career, I've gained great financial success,
and I've found myself at the precipice of total bankruptcy. I have come
from the satisfaction of living the American dream, with a young
family, a beautiful house, and a life of luxury, to the ruin and shame
of moral compromise and lost integrity. I have won and lost much on
my own, but it's been in my surrendering to God a decade ago that
I have gained the most. I have lived the gospel redemption story for
real. Through it all, I have gained a deep and profound faith that God
can literally fix *anything*. So when my daughter's life unraveled before
my eyes, although I was shaken, I was confident that if I could hear
God, he would provide the answer. It was up to me to listen carefully
and then have the courage to obey.

Personal Delusion or Divine Inspiration?

When I broached the idea of a family road trip to Paige, I expected
her to be skeptical. After all, this trip had all the earmarks of one of
my wild-goose chases, with only a few hints of confirmation that God
had actually given me the idea to help us reconnect as a family. I was

pretty sure that I had heard God on this, but I had no clear-cut Bible verses to share with my wife that promised a solution was going to be found somewhere along the way. I just sensed it was true.

To Paige's credit, she didn't dismiss my idea as ridiculous, although she must have been tempted. Instead, she prayed about it for several weeks. When she finally brought it up with me later, she was willing to go. So we began to plan this unprecedented family road trip for the summer ahead. We had about five months to get ourselves ready and figure out the details. We invited my brother and his family of five to share in the adventure, as his kids would also be on summer break from high school and college. We even included my seventy-year-old parents, convincing them to fly into Canada and meet us for a week at Lake Louise, Alberta. It would be an extended and multigenerational family vacation, a trip to remember for everyone.

Initially, the kids were stoked! They had never been to Canada and were very excited at the prospect of seeing mountains and the American West. In time, as they looked at maps and discussed the trip with each other, it dawned on them that the beauty of the North and West was only accessible after a 2.5-day, 1,800-mile drive across the flattest and most uninteresting terrain known to man. They also realized that the stuff that Dad enjoyed on a road trip might not be the same stuff they would enjoy. Their reaction was a mixed bag, with optimism and adventure edging the balance in favor of this wild idea.

When Paige and I agreed to go forward with our plan, I took a deep breath and let it out slowly. Either God was indeed up to something unique and supernatural in our lives, or I was insane. Either he was in this crazy idea and divinely preparing us to personally discover what we so desperately lacked, or it was an audacious and expensive diversion I had created in my head to satisfy my own need to take action.

I was mostly sure it was God. I believed deep down that it was his idea more than mine, that he had intentionally created a divine road map for our recovery, and that he had specific things to reveal to each one of us—things we would only be able to experience on our upcoming journey to the wilds of Canada and back. Paige and I began praying for God to reveal himself to our kids on the trip. We prayed specifically that he would teach Jessica to trust him wholly, that he would heal Bethany completely from her struggles of the previous year, and that he would help Caleb in his transition from boy to young man. We had hopes that he would work mightily in each child's life, but we left the details to him.

I was exhilarated, thrilled, and scared to death. I knew that the potential for another relational disaster existed. The possibility that our kids would tear each other apart before we made it out of Tennessee was real. I also knew that our marriage could become so stressed by the cramped quarters, constant interaction, and inevitable irritations over those thousands of miles that any recovery we might have gained as a family would be offset by new wounds in our marriage, inflicted on ourselves along the way.

God would have to be in this, or we would run the risk of making a bad situation even worse. I was fully relying on him to make it all work out. At first I wondered if I was supposed to share some deep and profound spiritual truth or life-changing principle on the drive out, or if we needed to read through a new Christian book as a family. But slowly I became aware that God didn't want me to do much at all on this trip. He just needed me to yield to his leading, and he confirmed he would give me the words to share along the way at just the right times.

I felt a sense of warning as well—a caution not to attempt to control my conversations with my kids, but to allow them to bring things up to me whenever they wanted. I also felt God suggesting that when my kids did come to me, I should be careful not to over-teach a point but simply seek to spend time with them in the moment and let God work in their hearts. That would be difficult for me. I was used to doing things, not just watching and waiting. But God spoke firmly and clearly to me on this point: *Brad, don't overthink this trip. Don't try to manipulate or contrive a special moment to really "win" your kids' hearts. Stay out of it. Let me do my eternal work in their lives my way and in my time!*

SIX

NASHVILLE TO SOUTH DAKOTA: AN ANXIOUS AND STORMY START

The reason why many are still troubled, still seeking, still making little forward progress is because they haven't yet come to the end of themselves. We're still trying to give orders, and interfering with God's work within us.

A. W. TOZER

Saturday, June 19, 2010, 4:30 a.m.—Time to Go

The road trip started early for my brother and his family, who drove to our place in Nashville from their home in Raleigh, North Carolina, so we could caravan up to Canada together. My brother, Kevin, is nine years older than I am and works as a senior computer engineer.

(He's smart.) He has been married for more than twenty years to Judy, and they have three kids: David, who was in his third year of college at the time, and twins Colleen and Suzanna, who had just graduated from high school and were about to leave the nest. My brother and I had been close over the years, and our kids had grown up with each other—cousins blending into close personal friendships. This trip was to be shared in part by us all, which meant the adventure was doubled. Kevin and his family would join us for over half the trip but would return home another way.

When they arrived, we were ready to load up the vehicles. Packing for a two-week-long trip requires some planning. We knew we would be in the wilderness area of Alberta and British Columbia for five days. In the summer heat of Tennessee, all we needed were shorts, T-shirts, and flip-flops. But considering the weather forecasts for Lake Louise, Alberta, it seemed we might need some sweaters and light jackets for the evenings and jeans and long-sleeved shirts during the day. Combine that with the hiking I had planned with my brother, and each of us would need hiking boots and tennis shoes as well. I took my full-size REI backpack and my camera gear as well as some pillows, blankets, and sleeping bags. We had reserved two cabins by Lake Louise, but we weren't sure whether we needed to bring our own bedding. But with the 2,500-mile drive, we assumed a few extra sleeping supplies would be useful no matter what we discovered in Canada.

We had mapped out a basic schedule for navigating the quickest route up to Canada from Nashville, and the plan called for a lot of hard driving the first two-and-a-half days. We had to average about nine hundred miles a day to get there in time to check into our rented cabins. Kevin had taken the time to study the maps and travel options available. He recommended a northerly route up through

Kentucky, Illinois, and Missouri across to western Iowa and then into South Dakota. That seemed as good a route as any to me, and it would allow us to see Mount Rushmore on the way—something none of us had ever been able to do before. So our path was set, and we rose before dawn to get an early start on our journey.

In the humid summer heat, afternoon thunderstorms are common across much of the Midwest and Great Plains states. This day would prove to be no exception. By early afternoon we had made it to eastern Missouri on Interstate 70 and were heading west at a brisk clip, one Toyota minivan and one Honda Pilot SUV crammed to the gills with anxious and excited family members. The adrenaline was still pumping from the anticipation of the trip, and everyone was in great spirits. So far things had gone well with our teenagers, and we were enjoying each other's company as we traveled toward Kansas City.

Wary of Weather

Caleb noticed it first . . . the sky was darkening in the west. Heavy, low storm clouds covered the sky across the entire horizon, creating an early dusk. Lightning flashes winked on and off in the distance, too far away to be heard or felt. It was evident from our vantage point that a significant thunderstorm was directly in our path. When you're traveling with kids, storms create more anxiety than when you're driving solo. Our teens were not panicky, but they were aware enough to know that a tornado was not out of the question for this time of the year.

Paige starting tuning our radio, looking for local news coverage so we could find out if any severe weather warnings had been issued for the area we had to drive through. Some had. Only a few minutes before, large hail and damaging winds had been reported in the town directly ahead of us. I tightened my grip on the wheel and checked my lights to make sure all was in order for what would surely be a heavy downpour. Traffic was starting to slow, and the first drops of rain began to ping off our windshield and hood. I wasn't concerned; I had driven through so many thunderstorms before that I had a good idea of what to expect and how to handle just about anything that might come up. I was confident and unafraid. I wasn't ignoring the conditions, but I wasn't turning back either.

In five minutes the weather had gone from threatening to seriously nasty. Rain fell in sheets across the road; cars were pulled off on the shoulder or parked under bypass bridges along the way. Wind buffeted our SUV as fifty- to sixty-mile-per-hour gusts raked across the open plains of Missouri. There was no cover, nothing to stop the storm's full fury from hitting us on the exposed highway. The kids were no longer calm.

I noticed a truck-stop billboard ahead and decided it might not be a bad idea to just pull off and wait out this downpour. We followed a line of slow-moving trucks and fellow travelers edging their way off the highway and into the truck stop. The wind was picking up; signs were beginning to buckle, and the larger truck trailers were swaying back and forth. The sky had gone from a dark purple to black, and the lightning and thunder were almost constant. We were going to get soaked even running the few yards from the parking area to the truck-stop restaurant. Due to lightning static, I couldn't get a channel on the radio, and my kids were starting to worry out loud if we might need to find shelter from a tornado. I encouraged them that we could find out more inside and that there might be a sturdy area where we could go if a funnel cloud were spotted nearby.

I was only suggesting that to help them feel better; I didn't really think we would have to use it. Meanwhile my nephew, David, had his smartphone out and was downloading the latest weather radar. Two tornadoes had been spotted within a few miles of our location, and several bands of heavy rain were on the way. This storm was not going to be over anytime soon. We took the opportunity to use the restrooms and fill up on some snacks and junk food. Hundreds of people had crammed into a small food court to take shelter. We were all watching the local television and news broadcasts to get the latest on the storm warnings.

Weather has always been a big deal in our family. I can remember my grandfather talking on and on about the different storms he had lived through as a kid—blizzards in Indiana and tornadoes in Illinois. He told stories of buildings, farms, and even entire towns that had been destroyed by the ferocity of a tornado, with many lives lost. Even so, those storms seemed too far away to matter. Now we were only a few miles from finding out for ourselves. My kids were trying to smile and laugh about the whole thing, but I could tell that they were genuinely afraid. This was not a good omen.

Fighting through the Fear

When Jessica, Bethany, and Caleb were very little (ages four, three, and two), we lived in east-central Illinois where spring tornadoes are a way of life. The flat prairies are defenseless against the wind and storms as they sweep in from the north and west, ripping their way through one small farm town after another. One spring evening we had to get into our home's crawl space to take cover from a twister that was a few hundred yards from our house. The space was dark and dusty with cobwebs and mold. We huddled together with a flashlight and some crackers and blankets while the storm raged outside. I remember the wind blowing so hard that the walls started to vibrate and the entire structure began humming like a giant tuning fork.

Our ears popped as the pressure dropped dramatically. I expected to look up and see nothing but open sky above us. We were saved that day—the tornado unexpectedly skipped over us and disappeared into the night as quickly as it had come.

The kids had never forgotten that day, and neither had I. A tornado is scary. Anyone who gets a thrill from watching the storm chasers on TV needs to understand the awesome, destructive power of a storm like that and reconsider how "fun" it might actually be when you get close. Our whole family had developed a strong aversion to bad thunderstorms, and my kids had carried that anxiety with them for years.

Ten-plus years later, here we were sitting on the dirty plastic chairs of a run-down truck stop. We were trying to act normal, sipping coffee and eating french fries while the wind and rain drummed across the windows and obscured everything beyond a few yards from our view. Going back out into that weather was going to be difficult for our kids to do, but if we were to move forward and get to Canada on time, we had to.

We considered our options. Yes, the storms were a threat, but not more so than staying in this rickety old building. We decided to drive on and take our chances. So with some foot-dragging and anxious looks, the kids climbed back in our Honda Pilot and off we drove into the unnaturally dark afternoon.

By the time we made it to the outskirts of eastern Kansas City, we had lost all our euphoria about the thrill of being on the road. Hours of relentless driving rain and a constant risk of hydroplaning on the wet interstate pavement had worn us all down. Constant delays from slowing and congested traffic and weather-related car accidents had put us way behind on our planned timetable for the first day. We finally took the exit for Interstate 29 North and slowly drove out of the storms into a late evening sunset on the left-hand side of our vehicle. The sun illuminated the foggy condensation beading up inside our windows as the endless fields of green flowed by like a rolling river. The sky's beautiful pink hue slowly faded, surrendering to the night. Summer sunsets in June are some of the best, since the days are near the longest of the year. And against the Midwest's open horizon, you can really see the full range of colors in the sky, as the evenings end moist and full of friendly cricket calls.

My kids were not fading as fast as I had expected. Red Bull and Starbucks coffee had amped them up enough to stay quite animated for the evening's drive north. Paige, however, was quickly running out of energy and had started to pile up her blanket and jackets to make a pillow on the passenger-side front door. She was relaxed, allowing me to drive as fast as I liked to make up for lost time, and I was not taking that for granted. We were cruising at a not-so-safe eighty-five miles per hour as we hauled up the back side of Iowa and into a series of brand-new roads and unexplored country. I was in my element and enjoying the drive as I began to review the day's events in my mind.

Reflecting

I hadn't seen any sign yet that God was moving in my kids' hearts. No, there hadn't been any major fights, but I could see that the thrill was quickly fading. The coming days could be rough. I saw Bethany listening to her iPod, lost in her own world. Caleb had chosen to ride in the third-row seat and had created a nice comfy spot for himself, nestled among the extra bags and suitcases. Jessica was gamely holding on, watching the sunset and reading a book as we silently rocketed across the nearly deserted roadway.

A few cross words had been shared, but the bigger problem was that more sarcasm had been flying around the cabin of our SUV than ever before. It was as if the kids had just discovered the joy of intelligent insight used as a weapon to humiliate each other. What fun. I hated it.

I was considering the whole put-down style of comedy that had become the mainstay of teen and preteen entertainment for years. There wasn't anything profoundly bad about those programs on Disney or Nick Jr., but the humor was always cloaked in some demeaning sarcastic punch line, always delivered by the acne-free pop icon actress or actor with spot-on timing and comedic pitch. After years of cable babysitting my kids, they had started to mimic what they had been taught. I didn't like it. No one had one nice thing to say to anyone else, and no one wanted to be vulnerable enough to stop the comebacks. The result was a constant barrage of one-liners jabbed back and forth at each other all day, everyone giving as well as they had received for hour upon hour. Nothing crass or vulgar was shared, nothing evil or twisted or perverse, but the spirit of it all was cold and unfeeling. It wasn't how a family should talk to each other . . . but it was so very common with popular television sitcoms, friends, classmates, and now in our home.

My Family Weighs In

Throughout this next portion of the book, I've inserted excerpts from my kids' journal of our trip to Canada and back. I hope these snippets of their perspectives on the events of our travels are fun for you to read. The journal notes were kept by Paige and the kids without any prior knowledge of this book whatsoever, so their reflections are spontaneous and unrestrained.

> **CALEB (13)**—*I was so happy to be with our cousins. It was boring driving, and I switched with my cousin Colleen so I was in the car with Suzanna for a while. Also when we were in Missouri, it*

stormed and tornado sirens went off. I FREAKED! Then we went into a Wendy's at a gas station.

BETHANY (14)—*Not too much happened on that day. We just traveled around from state to state. Got caught in a storm, which wasn't entirely fun. . . . Caleb had a spaz attack! Enjoyed spending time with our cousins.* ☺

JESSICA (15)—*We had a long first day! It was exciting to be on the road! Not much happened that day, it was just a lot of traveling. . . . [And she noted with an arrow over Bethany's journal entry] Bethany also spazzed.*

PAIGE—*Left at 4:30 a.m. We drove 1,000 miles today and were in six states: TN, KY, IL, MO, IA, and SD. We saw Omaha, NE, from a distance. We stayed the night in Sioux Falls, SD.*

Coincidence or Confirmation?

While I was musing about the day, I considered the nature and timing of the day's severe weather. It seemed weird how the storm had come up so suddenly like that. No weather forecasts had cautioned us until we were right up on it. One minute things were bright and sunny, and the next minute it was storming so hard that we had to pull off the road. As I drove and thought, I realized that, in a way, that's how things had happened in our lives.

One day Paige and I were cruising through our scheduled appointments: work, school, meetings, church, then home for a quick dinner, some last-minute e-mails, and some quick time to hang with the kids. Then we climbed wearily between the sheets to do it all again tomorrow—until the night we found our teen daughter crying in despair, and we knew something serious had gone wrong. Suddenly the life we thought was all planned out came to a grinding halt.

No longer were we feeling safe and predictable and sunny. A severe storm had suddenly snuck up on us, and we were left wondering how we'd missed the warnings.

The day's events seemed like a strange, live illustration of the night we found out about Bethany's molestation and dangerous depression. We were driving along in our lives without a care in the world, and then suddenly we were off track and behind schedule, seeking shelter from the storm that threatened our lives. Whether it's severe weather or a personal crisis, we all have two choices when we face a storm: We can stay where we are out of fear of the dangerous unknown, or we can take a risk and fight through our fear to push on. Staying put feels like the safe choice, but it's also a choice not to grow, a choice to hold on to our fears. When we stay in hiding, we're saying that our only goal is to keep things from getting worse. But that's not the purpose God has for our families. When we take a step into the unknown, we're acting out of faith—faith that God is with us; faith that he can do immeasurably more than we ask or imagine; faith that he can not only keep things from getting worse but can redeem the whole situation so entirely, so deeply, that someday we'll look back with amazement at all he has done.

That day on the highway, we didn't make the "safe" choice. We chose to push on and resume our journey as a family . . . together.

SOUTH DAKOTA TO MONTANA: THE "FOUR CHINS" TO TORNADO ALLEY

Travel, in the younger sort, is a part of education; in the elder, a part of experience.   FRANCIS BACON

Sunday, June 20, 2010—A Change of Scenery, a Change of Pace
Sioux Falls, South Dakota, is a nice town . . . or so I've heard. We didn't stay long enough to find out. We did notice the much cooler weather (seventy degrees vs. ninety-plus degrees in Tennessee) and the broad horizon stretching westward over the vast and lonely prairie. We left before sunrise. Six hours of sleep was all anyone had needed. The adrenaline and excitement bubbling in us was better than a dozen cups of coffee.

The weather was clear, cool, and sunny. After weeks of sweltering heat and humidity in Nashville, we were pleasantly surprised to dig out our windbreakers and sweatshirts to start our day. The car was humming with the buzz of anticipation. Caleb was the most excited because our day's plans included a stop at Mount Rushmore. He had learned about it in grade school and had been asking to visit it ever since. When he first heard of the national park, he was so young that he had mistakenly called it the "four chins," so that became its nickname and a family inside joke.

On the map it looked like the drive from Sioux Falls to Mount Rushmore was only a couple of hours. It wasn't. Well over six hours and almost four hundred miles away, it took "forever" to drive across some of the most desolate landscape in the lower forty-eight states. The scenery revealed the sheer size and scope of the vast American West in a way the kids had never seen before. At the few exits we passed on Interstate 90, we saw state historical signs for wagon-train exhibits, old pioneer villages with sod-house replicas, and aging fifties-era motels with run-down neon signs.

Everyone crashed hard after the first forty-five minutes, and soon the only company I had was my satellite radio. I was treated to the beautiful view of a warming sunrise lighting the flowing grasses of the plains. Cell towers, Wi-Fi, and the interconnectivity of suburbia were fading too, replaced by the occasional farmhouse, ranch, or barn as we sped westward to our destination.

Beyond a stop at Mount Rushmore for some sightseeing, the day's schedule included a serious race to Billings, Montana. After a careful review of the maps and distances, my brother and I deemed it "possible" that we could make it to our next stop in reasonable time. Our wives and the kids might have had something to say about this if they had understood just how long and grueling a drive we had planned.

But this early in the trip, we were all fresh and excited, so we bravely (and naively) pressed on.

My brother and I captained our steel-and-gas wagon train across the same path our pioneering forefathers had crossed only one hundred and fifty years before. We with the comfort of cushioned seats and air-conditioning, they with the sacrifices of blood and sweat and tears, riding on horses and wooden prairie schooners.

Our transportation would have been incomprehensible to the pioneers. In those days, a wagon train might cover eight to fifteen miles on a good day. In addition, the land was untamed, and there were no real roads—only ruts cut into the land, rough and rocky in dry weather and muddy up to the axles when it rained. Out here in the vast expanse of wild prairie, the settlers faced dangers that we didn't have to, like fatal skirmishes with Indian warriors, bandits, and rogue vandals, as well as wild animal attacks, perilous river crossings, and the simple risk of running out of food. It's difficult to grasp the courage and willpower of those early settlers in the 1800s who made the arduous, nearly yearlong journey to go west. Now here we were in 2010, covering over nine hundred miles a day without breaking a sweat, risking no more than cramped muscles and a sore behind.

The distances and the dangers must have seemed overwhelming to those families who chose to risk everything, including their lives, as they struggled to start anew in a distant land. The hazards we were facing were far different, but maybe our journey was similar in a symbolic way. I was leading my family on its own difficult path, from the safe and familiar to the new and unknown.

It had seemed so adventurous, so exciting to take a week and a half off from work before the Fourth of July, pack up the family, and sing our way happily into the sunset of our westward pilgrimage. Now I wasn't so sure. Snoring and morning breath were filling my Honda's pristine interior, as my unconscious family slept soundly. Reconnecting with my kids was not going to be easy.

Slowly we left the grasslands behind us and watched as the landscape gradually lost its green and started shifting subtly into the duller shades of brown and gray. The sky was endless above, blue with wispy clouds barely there, but visible if you really looked. The South Dakota Badlands were being heralded by every roadside sign and exit we passed. The pictures looked like a sci-fi movie set for the moon—cratered, irregular, barren expanses of rock and brush and dirt, eerie and yet beautiful. The area was known for its distinctive gold jewelry and pioneering history, and there was no shortage of roadside attractions tempting the teens to spend their carefully hoarded funds prematurely.

The most prominent of such trinketvilles was Wall Drug, a rambling "historical" structure with lots of old Western nostalgia for sale. The town of Wall, South Dakota, was seemingly being sustained by this one massive tourist trap still operating less than an hour from the more famous Badlands and Mount Rushmore. The racket I heard when we sped by without stopping was fierce. *Everyone* wanted to stop and see the acres of stuff; after all, for at least the past two hundred miles of interstate we had been reading sign after sign proclaiming the great deals on souvenirs and antique items offered at the Wall Drug establishment. No exaggeration—we'd seen at least fifty billboards of varying sizes, shapes, and colors. But we didn't stop. (You probably should, if you ever follow our route. My brother stopped the next week on his way back east. He purchased some nifty knickknacks for us to share and said it was really fun for the kids.)

I knew how important it was for us to keep to our schedule, and I chose to press on and save our time for the more memorable US monument at Mount Rushmore. I was glad we did. Soon we

approached one of our nation's greatest landmarks—the massive pro-
files (chins) of four of our greatest presidents, carved right into the
side of a mountain.

The "Four Chins"

Mount Rushmore seemed smaller than the images on TV, and from
the parking lot it looked less impressive than we thought it should
be—that is, until we climbed the hundreds of steps to see it up close.
It's huge. Beautiful, in fact, and a major photo op for any family.
We moved along the flag-lined walkway up to the stony viewing
overlooks, where we read about its creation and formation. It was
fascinating, and of course the kids were stoked to see where the movie
scenes from *National Treasure: Book of Secrets* had been filmed.

My wife was captivated by the history behind the European sculp-
tor who had the vision for creating such a masterpiece out of solid
rock. Many insightful brochures, books, short films, and artifacts
housed in the museum were interesting enough for history buffs to
stay an entire day and not get bored. We spent about an hour there.

The kids were like caged animals just released from their pens—
laughing, joking, snapping pictures with their cameras and smart-
phones everywhere they went. It was new, different, and exciting
for everyone. Not one of us had ever been to see Mount Rushmore
before, and we were experiencing it for the first time . . . together.

Bethany and her cousins enjoyed the view and took pictures from
the overlook, but she quickly migrated back to the visitor's center and
massive modern gift shop. Caleb was running from one display area
to another, snapping pictures, hamming it up with his sisters, and
generally having the time of his life. After all, this was "his stop" on
the adventure. The "four chins" had been his idea, his dream since
elementary school. He had a blast, and Paige and I bought a couple of

historical books on the site and story behind it all for Caleb to enjoy long after the trip was over.

Normally a reserved conversationalist, Caleb showed an impressive diversity of adjectives and exclamations as he tried to describe all he liked about Mount Rushmore. This was a side of him I hadn't seen in a few years. It warmed my heart to watch as the smile on his face lit up the entire room. Here was something we had driven for two days and over fifteen hundred miles to reach, and it had been worth it. That's a rare experience for a preteen anymore, with all the hype and sensationalism of our culture. Caleb, like many of his peers, had taken a cynical approach to things Paige and I wanted him to try or do, but this was different. He had found something that had exceeded his expectations. He had fulfilled a lifelong dream to see the monument at Rushmore firsthand.

I imagine God wants each of us to have the kind of moment that Caleb did—with the joy of hope fulfilled, dreams accomplished, and hearts made full. This was one life moment that really did satisfy, and it seared itself indelibly into my son's heart and mind in a way he will never forget. It's an experience that is all his, tangible and real and perfect. That's something preteens desperately long for, especially those like Caleb with older siblings who always reach the good stuff first. Jessica and Bethany had never allowed their younger brother to have the satisfaction of being an equal, but Mount Rushmore changed that for all of them. Caleb was now an "equal," at least on this trip. He had been there for their first view of the monument, and he had walked the same paths his sisters had. He was gaining on them, in life, confidence, and experience.

For Caleb, Mount Rushmore was more than a monument to four great presidents from the past. It was a symbol of his coming of age, of stepping out of the shadow of being someone's little brother and into the path of becoming his own person. I was proud and excited to see him completely content after visiting his cherished "four chins." Earlier in the day I'd had doubts about this trip, but here already I could see God working. I could sense that God had more in store, something special like this for each of my kids. Something designed to engage each of their hearts, to prove to them for life that he was close, intimate, and calling to them personally to come and follow after him.

It turned out that I was right. Those moments were coming for Bethany and Jessica too. But not before some more adventure and danger cropped up only a few hours later.

Montana Rest Stop

I've always told the kids that tornadoes occur only in the plains of the Southwest and Midwest portions of the United States. I was wrong. Turns out you can have tornadoes in Montana, and occasionally they have been known to form in the mountains, too.

The drive north and west of Mount Rushmore was mostly uneventful. We drove onward, avoiding the interstate for a shortcut—Highway 212, a great two-lane road that snakes its way northwest from South Dakota into Wyoming briefly and then deep into the rolling eastern hills of Montana. We were chasing the sun, racing westward on a nearly deserted road that rose and fell with each dip of the terrain. Pickup trucks and four-wheelers were about all we passed on the way. The sky was starting to darken far off in the west, but we paid it no mind, figuring those storms were fifty or more miles away.

The tall grasses and gradually rising plateaus of southeastern Montana are beautiful in their serenity and scope. Much like the South Dakota prairies, the landscape here seemed endless and unaffected by man, yet it was different, with deeper valleys and higher hills. We drove steadily higher as we cruised by abandoned farms and old mining towns. We began to see Indian reservation signs from time to time. Around the homes, beat-up trailers and old Chevys and Fords were rusting a slow death.

This was abject poverty in the countryside, and the kids had not seen anything like it before. With family in Memphis, Tennessee, and Raleigh, North Carolina, we had all seen what an urban ghetto looked and felt like, but this was different. Isolated, remote, alone . . . these people seemed to have no life in them. No desire. They lived in squalor and seemed almost content with it. Far from the frenzied atmosphere of city life and crime, these outposts of civilization were quiet and frozen in time. Everything felt old and moldy.

My daughters were more aware than they let on. The car was silent as we slowed from cruising speed to city speed, driving from one nearly vacant reservation town to the next. Eventually someone had to use the bathroom. The next stop was a nameless Indian reservation much like the dozen we had passed before. No McDonald's, no rest area, no 7-Eleven or Quik Stop; these were mom-and-pop gas stations and grocery stores. Made of wood, recycled metal junk, and steel, they looked like something out of a third-world setting.

We all entered a store, more out of curiosity than out of a desire to be there. It was cramped, old, and as worn inside as it was outside. The wary Native Americans working behind the counter could see what we needed. The oversize key to the restroom was handed over, and I began to peruse the shelves to find something for us to munch on as we trucked on to Billings, Montana, for the night.

I found some snacks, soda, and candy. We paid at the ancient manual cash register and wandered out. I thought Paige and the girls would surely be done by now, but no one was around. As I looked around, I saw trash, dirt, and battered remains of vehicles in every direction. Rangy dogs with missing teeth and bald patches in their fur were carefully watching my every move, whether from hunger or fear I couldn't tell. This place was definitely beat-up. I had seen my share of down-and-out small towns in my travels, from the old coal-mining towns of West Virginia to the abandoned cattle towns of rural Texas, but this was different.

My girls came to the car in a hurry, looking flustered. "Come on, Dad! *Come on!*"

"Okay, okay, I'm coming. What's the big hurry?"

"That bathroom back there was filthy," said Jessica.

"And we still need to pee," Bethany added.

"Oh man, are you kidding me? You girls didn't go in there?"

"Nope, Dad, it was so disgusting—really nasty and dirty, and there were live roaches and rat droppings. We just couldn't do it," said Jessica.

"We have to go on to the next town," said Bethany. "Or worst case, we'll go in a ditch by some trees if we have to."

Paige had already tried to convince them to use this bathroom, but they would have no part of it. I could tell by their reaction that this decision was firm, so I sped off out of town, careful to avoid any wandering animals or the dozens of extra-large potholes that dotted the cracked road. I was not surprised by my daughters' reaction; both of my girls had lived in relative comfort for their entire lives. Now in their high school years, they were growing into complex-thinking, opinion-breathing creatures who spat fire and had razor-sharp words for teeth. They knew what they liked and what they didn't, and they articulated that with a strength that was sometimes venomous. No amount of persuasion could change their minds. This worn-out, broken-down Cheyenne Indian reservation town was *not* on their list of fun, new places to visit.

We found another restroom thirty miles later, near Interstate 90 just south of Hardin, Montana. Complete with a Shell multi-pump modern gas station, it was much cleaner and more familiar. As I set to work refilling the SUV and wiping off the bugs and dirt from the windshield, I noticed a strange coolness in the air. I could see the line of ragged peaks off to the west. We had finally made it to the mountains! I was stoked. The Rocky Mountains are like old friends; I feel at home when I'm near them. Stretching from British Columbia, Canada, southward to Mexico, these mountains form the spine of the American West and divide the nation into eastern and western parts. This is why I had come. These mountains and their indescribable beauty were what I loved; this is what made my heart sing! The wildness of their ragged peaks and the allure of their rugged terrain made me come alive. They had drawn me to come back again and again, for dozens of road trips and adventures. But this was my first visit with my entire family along, and I was starting to allow myself to get excited. It was only a few hours to Billings, or maybe, if we made great time, Great Falls, Montana. We could crash after a long day, and then we would be off and up into Canada. We had really made it. Our goal was less than twenty-four hours away!

Dark Skies

I failed to notice how dark things were to the north of us. The skies ahead were turning black near the mountain peaks. It seemed a thunderstorm had built up during the day and was about to dump some serious moisture on the Rockies—and maybe soon on us.

Since we had been through the thunderstorm in Missouri only the day before, I knew Caleb and Bethany would likely be getting a bit nervous. So I took the time to reassure them that it was safe; nothing like a tornado would or could form this close to the mountains. I repeated what I had learned from the Weather Channel with my best reassuring voice: tornadoes don't form this high up; they are spawned only by a convergence of cold and warm fronts, something that the Great Plains are notorious for. This was just one of hundreds of daily short, intense thunderstorms that build up in the summer heat around the mountains. It was only dangerous if you were out hiking or above the tree line, not on I-90 heading into Billings for a hotel room.

Ten minutes later I saw a dark, wide cloud that seemed to be lowering onto the valley floor ahead of us. Then I noticed it was slowly rotating. *Wait, that couldn't be a tornado, could it?* Unfortunately, I didn't just think that last part—I said it out loud. Caleb and Bethany *freaked*. Both of them had battled a lifelong fear of tornadoes and storms, and they were wary of any severe weather reports on our local television. We had learned to keep them from knowing if there was in fact a threat, but our home in Tennessee had a great basement with lots of space to take shelter in, if we ever needed to.

The Honda Pilot was great, roomy, and safe for driving, but not much defense against the half-mile-wide tornado bearing down on us. I slowed to the roadside and saw that other cars were pulling off as well. People had already noticed that this storm was more than just thunder and lighting. My brother pulled off in his minivan and ran up to my window. "Bro, I've been flashing my lights at you for a mile. There is a *tornado warning* for Billings, Montana!"

If my kids hadn't been panicked before, this did the trick. Caleb started to howl like an animal trapped in the slaughterhouse; he was sobbing uncontrollably about death and dying and why we had to go on this trip anyway. Bethany was nearly as upset. She was wailing softly and rocking back and forth as she watched the storm's path a few miles in front of us. There was nothing we could do. To our left was a wall of granite—the base of the mountains that stretched for miles along the western slope. To the right was a stand of trees, a fence, and some gradual sloping fields of grass with no shelter, overpass, culvert, drainpipe, or a single structure to hide in, under, or around.

We couldn't turn around. We were just at the top of a rise in the interstate, and we couldn't reverse or cross the double lanes without risking being T-boned by a semi or another vehicle barreling over the rise of the hill at the legal limit of seventy miles per hour. We were stuck; we would just have to wait this one out. For Caleb, that wasn't good enough. He went into a hysterical hyperventilation fit about how stupid it was to just sit here and wait for the storm to rip us apart. Bethany agreed with Caleb, and Jessica was trying to calm them both down. Paige got upset at their refusal to be comforted and told them all to calm down, be quiet, and start to trust us as their parents. She told them we were aware of the situation and would take the proper precautions for everyone's safety when we could. Until then, we should pray. Wow, talk about stressful!

About that time my nephew, David, walked up to our SUV with his smartphone in hand and showed me the live radar map for the area. The good news was that the storms seemed to be moving north and east, slightly away from us. The bad news was that there were several tornadoes spinning off the big one ahead, and they were not moving in the same direction as the main supercell.

I joined in the fervent family prayers being whispered around me: "Jesus, we need your protection and peace right now. Please keep that storm from harming us and anyone else. Please show us the best way out of this mess and grant us the courage to trust your leading. Amen." Caleb started to calm down. Bethany began to recover as well and then encourage Caleb that things would be okay. Jessica was fine; she had started snapping pictures of the storms. It was like someone had just let the atmosphere of pressure and fear slide out of our vehicle. "Thanks, Jesus," I prayed.

I continued to watch intently as the storms seemed to hover over what I thought must be Billings and then slowly move away to the north and east. David's phone showed another line of strong storms heading our way, so we resumed our drive into Billings. Ten minutes later we saw the destruction.

Billings had gotten nailed by a freak tornado—the first in over fifty years, according to the local news. Pieces of buildings were lying on the main street; poles and trees and roofs were missing; the electricity was out; debris and glass and pieces of people's belongings were scattered for blocks. The storm had flattened a regional civic center, and its stadium-style roof was ripped back as if it had been worked over with a can opener. Ambulances and fire engines were everywhere, and police and patrolmen of every stripe were redirecting traffic, helping survivors, and generally making sure everyone was okay.

It had been a matter of timing. If we had been ten minutes earlier getting into Billings, we might have been hurt. As it was, we were spared. The whole family was greatly affected by the near miss, and Caleb in particular was in shock. This was the first real danger he had ever encountered for himself, his first real sense of his own mortality. It was scary, exciting, and sobering all in one potent life moment. Bethany was quick to react and quick to recover. Jessica and Paige stayed restrained in their responses, but we all had to process the enormity of what we had just witnessed. It's one thing to read about tornadoes or watch some footage on the Weather Channel, but it's another thing entirely to see one firsthand and realize how dangerous and unpredictable they really are.

After checking in at a Holiday Inn Express (without electricity), we dove into our dark rooms weary, worn, and slightly exhilarated.

We had seen some incredible sights that day—some man-made and some natural. I don't even remember taking my clothes off before slipping into a seven-hour coma.

As I slept, I dreamed. I remember little of it, but I woke up with a profound feeling of being protected. I could almost hear God saying to me, "I kept you safe last evening. I will continue to keep you safe. Your family is in good hands. My grace is active in your lives, and I've been guiding your steps ever since you chose to come back to your wife eight years ago." It was as if he had whispered in my ear while I was sleeping. I kept hearing him remind me of the sacrifices Paige and I had made to put our family first. He said, "Because you didn't try to assume control of your lives again, I am leading your family forward to healing, to wholeness, to security. Just as I kept you from real danger yesterday in that tornado, just as your daughter didn't die in your home last fall, you will continue to be kept in the center of my protection. You and your family will grow close; you will encounter faith and love as you continue on this journey of life."

I don't normally have dreams. But Father's Day is only a once-a-year observance, and Sunday, June 20, had been that day. I was grateful for that most generous gift—the well-being of my family. It was another reminder that I was not solely responsible for my family's safety. God was in control. Now and forever, we were in his loving and capable hands.

Journal Entries:

CALEB—*That was a fun day. I remember stopping for lunch and having a picnic at the gas station. My sandwich was amazing; I thought I didn't like potato bread. Then a tornado formed in front of us in Billings. I hyperventilated, I think. I hate tornadoes. Then we found a nice Holiday Inn Express that had the power out that we stayed at. They had free cookies for us too. Also . . . Mount Rushmore . . . AMAZINGNESS!!*

BETHANY—*That was by far the WORST day of the entire trip. So we are driving down the road, right? And all of a sudden, BAM, we drive over a hill (outside of Billings) only to find ourselves a few miles from vicious rotating tornadoes and lightning flashes in the dark sky. Eventually we made it to a nice little Holiday Inn Express in Billings, MT. Went swimming and ate some yummy Applebee's for dinner.*

JESSICA—*This day was pretty awesome and scary! We watched a tornado form in Billings, MT, which scared us all to death. It was awesome because we got to drive across South Dakota, and I loved it! It was a pretty stressful day, but cool to look back on. We also went to Mount Rushmore, and it was awesome! I'm glad we saw the iconic "four chins."*

PAIGE—*We left Sioux Falls and drove across South Dakota to Mount Rushmore. It was a beautiful sunny day. Afterwards we headed to Montana through Wyoming on Hwy 212. We stopped at a convenience store near Colony, WY, to have a picnic in the parking lot. Uncle Kevin and Aunt Judy had packed things for sandwiches. We were hungry, and the food tasted great! The mosquitos were bad though. We had hoped to make it to Great Falls, MT, but ran into very bad weather outside of Billings. We finally were able to continue into Billings and quickly found a Holiday Inn Express for the night.*

EIGHT

MONTANA TO CANADA: RUNNING WILD AND FREE

God doesn't call us to be comfortable. He calls us to trust Him so completely that we are unafraid to put ourselves in situations where we will be in trouble if He doesn't come through.

FRANCIS CHAN, *CRAZY LOVE: OVERWHELMED BY A RELENTLESS GOD*

Monday, June 21, 2010

The day dawned bright and fair, with no sign of the previous day's storms. We took state Highway 87 north out of Billings on our way to Great Falls, Montana. Not the most direct route, but it went through Lewistown, a small ranching town close to the commonly traveled road. This was a stop we had all agreed to make. Kaycee Mantooth,

who had been the girls' youth leader at our church in Tennessee, lived
here. Recently relocated back to her hometown, she and the girls had
been Facebooking for weeks in anticipation of our trip to Canada.
We were determined to see her once more if we could. Lewistown
was one of only a few rural outposts that had a McDonald's, so we
met up with Kaycee there. We enjoyed our time with her immensely,
knowing this could be our last shot at some American Diet Coke and
good ol' Egg McMuffins for a while.

After a little time catching up with Kaycee, we resumed our drive
north to the border. The road was in good shape, and the sky above
us was clear. Yet the presence of thunderclouds building on the high
plains was evident across the horizon to our east. Caleb was uneasy,
questioning me about the weather forecast in Canada and the likeli-
hood of a tornado this far north.

I was honest with him. "I have no idea, son. But I do have a
profound sense of peace about the rest of our trip. I don't think
we're going to encounter any more tornadoes or dangerous thunderstorms." He seemed to accept what I had said and went back to iPod
land.

It was so frustrating to watch my kids engage with me and then
disengage. When they needed something or if we stopped for something fun or new, they came out of their techno-cocoons. But when
the need passed or we piled back in the car, things almost instantly
reversed course, and they tuned out again as quickly as they had
plugged in.

I really wanted to have some serious time with my girls. They were
growing up so fast. High school years, dating, boys, drugs, college,
politics, economics, global warming . . . man, we could really connect
by talking, by sharing ideas, debating, whatever. But all I got in the way
of significant conversation were a few mumbled acknowledgments of

thanks for the snacks we doled out along the way. My wife was enjoying herself at least . . . right? "Paige?" She mumbled a sleepy *um-hmm*
as she readjusted her pillow for better sleep.

By now I had memorized the entire playlist for the "80s on eight"
station on XM radio, so I listened to some news channels as I drove.
It wasn't long until we hit rain again. Clouds formed spontaneously
along both sides of the Interstate 15 corridor into Canada. I hoped
this rain would stop soon. Day two had about killed us, and day three
was not shaping up to be much fun. What had I gotten us all into?

The doubts began to form into accusations, which pounded into
my mind and heart with a relentless message of guilt and fear and
shame. It left me wondering if maybe God wasn't really that personal
or that connected with us. Still, there was something deeper here.
When the idea for this trip first came to me, I had *felt* God's presence.
I knew it was him. I couldn't give up now. We were almost there,
and God had promised that this trip would provide a way for us to
reconnect as a family. I would have to take it on faith that he would
keep that promise. But I had to whisper to myself, *No, we should
not stop this pathetic and self-centered road trip; it wasn't my idea. God
told me to take my family. It was his inspiration, not my own, so he will
definitely show up soon!*

Canada, eh?

After wrestling with this doubt for an hour, I noticed the clouds had
formed a ragged line, thanks to an emerging cold front—complete
with gusty winds, light hail, and heavy, window-smacking rain. It came
in sheets, darkening the sky to a dusty coal color, as I drove with my
lights on and my entire family passed out in boredom and fatigue
around me. We rolled sloshing into Canada as unceremoniously as
possible. Joining the traffic queue up to the border crossing, we waited

in the half-light of the thunderstorm and the dirty spray of road grease and grime. I felt a surge of excitement. *Woo-hoo! We're finally here!*

Our passports were reviewed. Twenty minutes and one open-window interview later, the Mathias clan of Spring Hill, Tennessee, was in a new country. We passed across the US border at Sweetgrass, Montana. It was encouraging to see the kids raise themselves from the piles of sleeping bags, candy wrappers, lumpy pillows, two-day-old sweatshirts, mangled blankets, and a web of personal electronics to put their shoes on and briefly get excited with me to be in a new country for the very first time! But that lasted about five minutes before they realized they were still trapped in our SUV staring at wet, boring grasslands.

I had made this crossing from the United States to Canada and back several times with my friend Brian. It was the site of one of our more unhappy memories—that of being detained by border guards for several hours in 2005 because of a paperwork mix-up. It happened in the early morning hours, when we approached the border with a mud-caked car after a thirty-six-hour, off-road impulse trip into Canada. It had been one of the most spontaneous, beautiful, and dangerous trips we had ever done. We had decided to drive up from Denver after a business conference there. Canada had looked closer on the map when we set out, and by the time we arrived back at the border at 2 a.m., we'd been driving dirt roads for days. We were unshaven and dirty, with old hiking clothes, bandanas, and dozens of old pop cans and junk-food wrappers littered throughout our rental SUV. For some reason the border guards decided we might be a threat and forced us to stop so they could search our whole vehicle in the dead of night. Several hours of questioning later, we were finally let go . . . but I kept this little memory to myself. I didn't dare share much about my bad border experience now; it would only make the kids nervous.

Few of us consider how risky it really is to leave your country of origin and journey into a foreign land. I mean, everyone in our family knew that the laws in Canada are different from ours, although the customs and habits of most Canadians would be very similar to ours. Still, the regions we would visit here would be distinct enough that we could see, hear, feel, and taste the differences. I had a profound hope that my kids would fall in love with the country as much as I had on my previous adventures to the Canadian Rockies. I love Canada; someday maybe I could stay. But for now, I was content to be a one-week visitor with my gang of five.

The kids gradually woke up as their need to find a bathroom grew stronger. The rain had not let up even a little. Water had puddled the roadways, parking lots, and ditches all along Highway 4 north to Calgary. The day never really seemed to get fully light. The storm was relentless, pounding the ground in waves, mildly thundering but mostly just soaking anyone who jumped out of our SUV for a desperately needed bathroom break.

Some people have a misconception that once you cross the border into Canada, the scenery suddenly changes. It doesn't. We drove several hundred miles in the rain, on roads remarkably like our own US Interstate system, only better and newer. The speed limit was in kilometers per hour instead of miles per hour, but because drivers use the same side of the road as we do in the States, the transition was minimal. However, the food, the gas, and the groceries were all new. Even when we saw familiar company names, the products were completely different. The kids loved that. They tried all kinds of new junk food, Canadian style!

What started to creep up on us was the lack of fast-food options. Canada loves A&W franchises—these diners are everywhere. They also have some McDonald's, although the menus are significantly different from ours. For the most part, Canadians move at a similar pace to their southern neighbors, but they seem to have a greater awareness of the need for moderation. So there tends to be less of everything. Fewer gas stations and restaurants, fewer malls, less trash, fewer people, fewer signs and hotels. I've learned that when traveling in Canada, it's always best to plan ahead for stops.

The weather was miserable. Usually driving up Highway 4 to hit Highway 2 into Calgary is a beautiful view—rolling wheat and ranchlands as far as the eye can see, with a growing line of ragged peaks off to the west, the northern version of the American Rockies. These peaks are stunning, glacier-filled and sparkling in the sunlight. Unfortunately, with heavy rain and low clouds, we couldn't see anything but the double-trailered semi in front of us and the smeared, rain-smudged windows on either side. My wipers were barely keeping up with the rain, so I slowed down to be extra cautious and watch for the unfamiliar roads and signs.

We got lost anyway.

Yes, that's right. We got lost. I almost remembered the right way from my last drive through the southwest outskirts of Calgary, but in the end I missed the turnoff. We took an extra ninety minutes going ten miles an hour in rush-hour, Monday-evening traffic. I was ticked off. Rain, traffic jams, construction everywhere . . . plus my GPS and XM Radio stations didn't work in Canada. I was fuming mad at myself, at my kids, and for some unknown reason at my wife for being so calm. I defensively reminded her that I had in fact chosen the right way; it just wasn't the fastest way. She knew better than to debate the point; she just nodded her head knowingly and smiled. "It's fine, honey. We'll get there all the same."

I hate it when a plan goes awry. I had hoped for us to be in our cabin at Lake Louise by now. My parents had flown in from Tennessee to meet us there, and dinner was probably sitting on some perfectly set table getting cold as my mom anxiously wondered what had happened to us. I could just imagine the phone call: *We're going to be late . . . like four hours late. Can you put all the food away, and we can start over when we get there?* It was frustrating to have come this far and still have such a long way to go. I wanted to be there and out of this seat for a change. We were going on three thousand miles in three days, and my backside was about to go on a seat strike.

Between the rain, the Canadian-chocolate taste fest, and the rocking of the car for thousands of miles, the kids had been hypnotized a bit. Thanks to spiked blood sugar, steady sounds of rain, low light, and numb extremities, they were drifting from conscious to unconscious to cope with the stress of three days and nights in a ten-by-ten box. Perhaps their napping was also a noble attempt to avoid manslaughter charges against their siblings. I was not so fortunate, so in my fatigue and impatience, I blew my top at my wife.

There we all were, riding along anxiously as we inched our way across Calgary and out toward the mountains in the west. I tried to regain some amount of confidence, mumbling to myself and to anyone who would listen that I really did know Highway 1 very well. If we could just find the exit to Highway 1, we would be good. It was impossible to get lost once you were able to find Canada Highway 1.

My brother's minivan was gamely trying to keep up with us as I kept bobbing and weaving my way through narrowing lanes of new construction and gridlocked traffic. *Man, this better be worth it,* I thought, huffing through my slowly grinding teeth and squealing tires. *I'm either going to get us to the mountain cabin soon, or I'm going to get detained again by the polite Canadian police for speeding. But no matter what, we're not staying in this mess.* I clenched my jaw and furrowed my brow in concentration. The kids understood the wisdom of leaving Dad alone when that Sasquatch profile came over me. I tightened my grip on the steering wheel, bullying and pressing my way forward.

Letting It Go

Somehow—I have no idea how—we suddenly emerged on the right highway, going in the right direction. A few minutes later, the sun started to break through the clouds, and the kids could see the mountains profiled on the horizon. I started to laugh. The moment of dark despair passed like it had never been there at all. I relaxed, blew out the breath I'd been holding, and started to trust that maybe God did have my back on this trip. Maybe I didn't have to worry about making sure everything went on schedule, just as planned, with perfect weather and good health for everyone along the way. After all, that was God's job anyway, right? I remembered my lingering dream impression from the morning and smiled.

As the Sasquatch in me disappeared, I pointed to the Calgary Olympic Park we drove by. We could see the massive ski jumps and bobsled tracks. Our kids kind of remembered the Calgary Winter Olympics back in 1988 and snapped some quick pictures through fogged windows. The sun and sights had started to rouse them from their lethargy. The sky was growing remarkably bright for being six in the evening, even for June, and then I remembered that not only were we driving west, but north. A lot north, in fact—so far north that the days were significantly longer than in the States. It was as light at 6 p.m. here as it was at 3 or 4 p.m. at home. The sun was going to be up until nearly 10 p.m., and its dusky glow would last until close to midnight. Life was looking up; maybe our first day in Canada could be revived a bit before it ended.

With renewed hope and encouragement, we pushed our way up

the foothills of the mountains, and I introduced my family to some of God's greatest work: Banff National Park. With breathtaking beauty and views of the unique mountains, rivers, and lakes, no other place I know of has the same scope and raw beauty as Banff. We avoided the temptation to constantly stop and take pictures on the roadside, opting instead to keep going and get over to the Baker Creek Chalets, check into our cabins, greet my parents, and drive the few miles to picturesque Lake Louise. We would soon be able to get out and explore the lake, soak in its amazing views of Victoria Glacier, feel the cool and calm turquoise waters, and stare at an impossibly beautiful castle hotel on its banks—all just as the sun set. Perfect! We had barely made it in time.

By some divine spark of inspiration, my entire family was now in Canada! We were about to spend a week in one of the most beautiful spots on the planet. I believed that God wanted us to be here, together, at this time for a reason. I just didn't have a clue what was supposed to happen next. And for the first time since climbing behind the comfy wheel of my Honda Pilot, I was genuinely okay with that.

Journal Entries:

CALEB—*I had a good day that day, but it was boring riding the whole day again. I was happy when we made it to Canada! Then we got to go to Moraine Lake, and it was fun skipping rocks (I was the best) in the lake. Though it was a late spring and there wasn't much water in it yet.*

BETHANY—*I loved seeing Kaycee! We had not seen her in a year, so catching up with her was lots of fun. When we arrived in Canada, everyone headed to Moraine Lake. It was beautiful there. I loved the clear lake water and trying to skip stones. Good day!*

JESSICA—*This day was great because we got to see Kaycee. We almost didn't get to see her because of the time, but Dad waited and we got to! It was great seeing her, and hopefully Mom and Dad will move out there! Ha ha, who knows? After that we crossed the border, and it was kind of intimidating. We made it through, though, and stopped in a little village while it was pouring rain to get Canadian candy! It was a GREAT day! I loved Canada and even the fact that the temperature was Celsius and the road speed was measured in kilometers. Plus Calgary was really cool and modern. That was a day just full of new experiences and excitement!*

A WEEK IN GOD'S COUNTRY AND THE HIKE THAT CHANGED IT ALL

God writes the gospel, not in the Bible alone, but on trees, and flowers, and clouds, and stars. MARTIN LUTHER

THE FIRST FULL DAY in Canada dawned early . . . 4:35 a.m. early. I was up, though. With my newly purchased hiking boots, REI backpack, and warm, layered climbing gear, I was ready for some alpine exploration. The kids were zonked. They had stayed up late into the night as they settled into their cabin rooms, hurriedly unpacking and shoving pictures, coupons, and tourist brochures at me as fast as they could read them, all promoting everything from river rafting and boat rides to guided tours, glacier excursions, helicopter sightseeing, horseback riding, shopping malls, and of course the local wildlife. Then they collapsed in their sleeping bags for the night.

They were exhausted from the three-day drive we had just made. Few have ever done that three-thousand-mile drive so fast, and fewer still with two vehicles and ten people. Now my brother's family and mine had met up with my parents, and the twelve of us were sharing two rental cabins, each complete with a porch, loft, two bedrooms, and kitchen. It was modern, cozy, and rustic all at the same time. The location was ideal, scouted out well in advance by my parents online. Our home base now placed us within a ten- to twenty-minute drive of Lake Louise, Moraine Lake, and the adjacent forests of Yoho National Park.

Kevin and I had each been working out for months to shed some accumulated middle-age belly fat. We knew the demands of strenuous activity at this elevation would be much harder than back home, and we made it our business to get leaner and meaner for this trip. Now thirty pounds lighter, we both were up and at it before anyone else. We didn't want to waste a second of daylight, so we hit the road at dawn, starting early so we could get back in time to take the family exploring before lunch. With full coffee mugs and plenty of gorp (a homemade hiker's mix of granola, trail mix, and chocolate candy), we drove straight to Lake Louise to beat the "sure to come" summer tourist crowds. We had purchased a hikers' trail guide long before we came, and we already knew by heart the basic mountain trails we wanted to explore.

Today's hike would be a "moderate" 8.5-mile climb (round trip) to the Plain of Six Glaciers.[7] We planned to stop at the summit for breakfast at the Lake Agnes Tea House, a tradition for serious hikers who make the pilgrimage to Lake Louise. Created by turn-of-the-century climbers and explorers for summer excursions, this old stone teahouse is accessible only by foot or helicopter. A small contingent of staff live there for the summer to serve visiting hikers basic breakfast and lunch fare and, of course, a broad assortment of English teas.

We were stoked, and our adrenaline rush beat back the fatigue of our three-day, three-thousand-mile drive. It was cold—three degrees Celsius, or about thirty-eight degrees Fahrenheit—and we could see our breath as we paused on the trail at the bottom of the mountainside. After skirting the edge of Lake Louise, this trail would wind its way up a modest slope. About three and a half miles later, it would top out, overlooking the Plain of Six Glaciers and the teahouse. My brother was intensely excited; he had been waiting to do this for months and had never had an opportunity to climb in this area before. He had heard of my adventures up here and had been quietly waiting for his chance to join me.

Morning Glory

We eagerly hit the trail and started our hike. It was quiet, calm, and magnificent. The turquoise lake water lapped along the trail's edge. Mist and fog hovered over its surface as the warmer water reacted to the chill of morning mountain air. Magical is the only word I can use to describe these glacier-fed lakes. With fresh glacier silt suspended in it, the water reflects the light and creates an unearthly blue-and-green sapphire color. Hiking near these lakes is like leaving the old world behind and entering into an alpine nirvana. It's indescribably beautiful and dangerous all in one moment, like escaping to Narnia or Middle Earth.

Lake Louise and its nearby cousin, Moraine Lake, are probably two of the most photographed bodies of fresh water in the Northern

Hemisphere. They are perfect in shape, color, and geography, surrounded by the towering Canadian Rockies, complete with patches of sparkling glaciers, including the iconic Victoria Glacier directly in front of the Lake Louise castle hotel. We were hiking up to the very bottom edges of that glacial field, and it was exhilarating to breathe the freshest air possible and peer up the sheer, rock-cliff walls on either side of us as we scanned their surfaces for rare wildlife along the way.

The exhilaration came not only from the panoramic vistas ahead, but also from the possibility of running into a native grizzly bear. In this glacier-fed valley and on these specific trails, grizzlies had been seen hundreds of times in the past decades. They posed well-documented, well-known threats to hikers' safety. Grizzly warning signs were posted on several trailheads we passed on our way up. Experts tell us that 99 percent of the time the bears avoid humans, but there is always the one percent that hikers have to consider. We carried little in the way of protection, other than our senses and a short-bladed forest knife.

Bears can move faster than horses and will outrun anyone who tries to flee. The brochure at the Banff park office suggested that if a bear moves to attack, you should lie down prone and cover the back of your head with your arms . . . *unless* you think the bear is hungry. If it's not just reacting to protect itself but being angry or aggressive, you should fight back at the bear's advance with all your might—the idea being that if you are successful, you might be able to make it go away and bother some other, less difficult prey. Those are some contradictory instructions for sure! The brochure said people would have to decide in a few seconds which kind of bear attack they were under and react accordingly. *Were they serious?*

I hoped we wouldn't find out.

The climb was exhausting, but it was worth every ache and pain in my forty-year-old joints. Once we passed the lower peaks, we could see the entire Bow River Valley, which ran down the center of Banff National Park. From our view in the clouds, it was a brilliant blue ribbon of water that snaked its way through the green wilderness and disappeared far in the distance. The peaks above us were inaccessible without climbing gear and a guide, so we didn't even consider going farther. Instead, we walked the few hundred feet to the teahouse and enjoyed some fresh tea and homemade hummus, veggies, and warm whole grain bread as we watched the forest wake up and the sky lighten with the full rays of early morning. What a way to welcome the day. I was ready to park here and not leave . . . ever. It was glorious!

Gone were the thoughts of bears, danger, or risk. They were replaced by happiness, joy, and contentment as I was reminded again how the beauty of God's Creation always restores my soul in ways I can't articulate. That's part of the secret I discovered in Canada.

Beauty and Transformation

Beauty is not dependent on our ability to grasp its significance. It can inspire us whether we are aware of it or not.

Beauty doesn't need our conscious appreciation of its soothing and transformational qualities for our hearts to enjoy its healing benefits. Oh no, divine beauty often sidesteps the mind's logical attempts to comprehend, process, and categorize information. Instead, it burrows directly into our hearts and souls, depositing its precious seeds of hope and glory and promise for change. Refreshing us and reminding us of God's unique and unparalleled artistry, its effect is to renew us from the inside out. Beauty is a reflection of the glory of God, and from his created works we get a partial view of the majesty, power, and transformational splendor that is part of our Maker. When we finally get away from the intellectual grind of work, schedules, and life, we slowly start to unclench our hearts. Our faith begins to rekindle, and most of us will eventually allow ourselves to relax in the presence of nothing but pure, holy, and undefiled glory. God's glory!

The beauty of nature refreshes my heart like nothing else. I always forget how powerful it really is. But once I'm there, soaking it in and feeling rejuvenated, I never want to leave. I want to experience it again and again and again. Like an addict looking for my next fix, I'm searching for one more glimpse of the divine beauty and artistry of my Savior. For me, those things are never more evident than in the glory of a mountain or an ancient glacier, in the shimmer of a lake, or in the pungent aroma of a fresh evergreen alpine world. Encountering those things moves me from just surviving my life to remembering that I was meant to be alive, thriving and growing and expanding.

The apostle Paul reminds us in Romans 1 of the overwhelming evidence of God's existence as revealed in Creation. There can be *no doubt* about the glory of a Creator in our world. For those who take the time to look, signs of God and his artistic passion abound. That's why I was so excited to get my kids out into this fantastic scenery. I wanted them to experience the glory of God's Creation for themselves, without my preaching at or pushing them. I wanted them to be renewed and refreshed simply by the peace and beauty around us.

Bow Falls

I could go on and on about the many memorable adventures we shared as a family that week in Canada. One of my favorites was when my brother and I discovered a mother and baby mountain goat (not bighorn sheep but very rare, endangered mountain goats) on a rock wall we hiked under one lucky morning. I could exhaust you with our tales of dozens of animal sightings—the many hundreds of elk, deer, and caribou, the brief glimpses we caught of a momma black bear and her cubs, or the beavers and raccoons that seemed to lope around fearlessly. We saw a couple of grizzly bears from the road (no closer, thank goodness), and it was awe-inspiring for us to observe their size and strength firsthand.

As we drove around Banff and Jasper National Parks, we did our best to take it all in. Every drive offered something new to marvel at. Even the ordinary roadside scenery was enough to cause us to stop from time to time and take another picture of the majestic nature all around us. We hurried from one spectacular glacier, overlook, and hike to another. For five full eighteen-hour days we climbed, hiked, shopped, and ate. As we explored, we photographed thousands of images, most of famous places along the Banff, Lake Louise, and Jasper valleys.

During the days we split up based on interests. Paige and my sister-in-law, Judy, liked to do some shopping, rest, and look through the local gift shops, while my parents joined in on the drives and short hikes as they could. But almost every night we had dinner together—all twelve of us, crammed into two small cabins with even smaller kitchens. Each of the kids helped with the dishes and meal prep, while the dads and boys were active fixing gear and vehicles and putting together provisions for our next day's adventures. My parents were thrilled. They had their entire family with them, and even if they couldn't do everything, we worked hard to include them in the touristy trips to see the sights, occasionally eat out at a local restaurant, or enjoy a short hike at nearby Lake Louise. It was chaotic but fun, and when my parents needed to retreat from the amped

atmosphere of six grandkids and four adult parents, they simply went
to bed or sat on the porch while we all dashed about.

Despite all the exploring and countless beautiful excursions we
enjoyed that week, one specific day and place defined our entire stay
for me. On the trail from Bow Lake to Bow Glacier Falls, something
special occurred. It became a pivot point for my family, a catalyst
for faith to grow, and the beginning of reestablishing the intimate
personal connections we desperately needed restored. It was a life-
changing hike to paradise, both literally and figuratively.

Kevin and I had scouted out the hike the day before and decided
to invite the kids to join us—never thinking they would, given the
very early start (4:30 a.m.) and a lot of exposure to cold and the elements. Yet all six kids jumped on board with the plan. We set out before dawn—Kevin, his three kids, me, and my three—ready to meet
the challenges ahead. A full six miles, this seldom-used trail back to
the falls would require fierce determination from all of us to reach its
summit. We knew the trip would include certain dangers. Grizzlies
were frequently seen in this valley, and loose shale rock rose steeply
on all sides as we climbed the sloped path. The narrow steps ahead
would require balance, courage, and stamina to climb successfully.
All the while we needed to avoid the freezing streams of glacial run-
off that crossed the path about every hundred yards. At times water
seemed to be on or near the trail everywhere, soaking our weary feet
in the frigid morning temperatures. We were well beyond the familiar, out of reach of technology and our usual creature comforts. We
had moved out of the safe and predictable and had entered into the
world as it was. As we climbed, we could feel the wild roaring edge
of civilization falling away behind us, and it felt great!

Hikers and climbers know how important layers of clothing,
waterproof jackets, and light gear are. Hiking in high country in the

late spring is an exercise in constant transition—from cold to hot and back again in eight hours. We were sweaty and cold, steaming and numb, wet and dry, and everything in between as we moved from the lower valley trail up into the rocky, thinning tree line. We were literally on the tops of several mountain peaks in the remote Canadian Rockies, and we knew the summer weather itself posed a significant threat, including the risk of afternoon lightning storms and the sudden sleet, snow, or rain squalls that were normal daily events. Kevin and I were well aware that if we wanted to survive in such an unstable climate and remote location, it was essential that we pay attention to our environment.

We walked past the cabins and the iconic Num-Ti-Jah Lodge. By now we were headed far away from the casual traveler's stroll or the guided tour highlights; we were backpacking into the remote Canadian wilderness carrying our own water, snacks, and lunch. We were committed to reaching the soaring glacier's edge, which in summer formed the magnificent Bow Falls that rose over five hundred feet in the far distance.

I hadn't been sure how the kids—definitely more comfortable in the safety of suburbia than in the rugged wilds of the Canadian Rockies—would react to the hike. Would they get tired or cranky? Would they lag behind? Would they complain about the lack of cell service or where the next rest spot would be? Not at all. I was amazed to watch them come alive as their eyes were opened to the power of the natural beauty around us.

All the kids were amped up from the new sights and sounds that surrounded us. Even my naturally reserved son, Caleb, was excitedly noticing the spectacular views and clean air as he picked up his pace, sensing that the goal of finding the falls ahead would be well worth the effort. My daughters and nieces were scrambling to get their cameras out in time to catch the various fleeting images of wildlife dodging our noisy approach. They were all truly waking up, maybe for the first time, as they began to realize just how special this place was. They knew how far they were from the normal civilized world, and it seemed to both excite and scare them. The threat of running into a grizzly bear or cougar was offset by the allure of other wildlife: seeing a bald eagle or an elk in the next bend of the river, or getting a quick glance at a scrambling bighorn sheep—or, ever rarer, a mountain goat—leaping across the steep rocky slopes that rose on both sides of our trail.

We were all experiencing nature the way it was intended to be: wild and wonderful. Not tamed by humans in any way, it was fresh, raw, and untainted by development or commercialization. It was impossible to miss the hand of the Creator on the artistic masterpiece surrounding us—the indescribable beauty of the glaciers and streams, untouched forests, and fragile alpine flowers struggling to bloom for a few days in the brief summer sunshine. God was everywhere, his presence more real here than in the hushed sanctuary of a modern church, and my kids were noticing. I watched in awe and appreciation as they soaked it all up and began to speak of the majesty and power of God to make something so surreally perfect just for us to enjoy. I couldn't have asked for a more exact answer to my prayers. God had led us all here, and he was speaking in a new and unexpected way. My heart was warmed, and tears formed at the edges of my vision as I thanked God for his flawless timing and mysterious ways.

How had this happened? I didn't recall any significant difference in the preparations we had made for this hike. We had been in Canada for three days now, and the routine had formed quickly: Go to bed late. Get up early. Hike, explore, eat, shop, crash, explore, eat again, and hit the sack. We had traversed the entire Bow Valley, voraciously eating up every possible experience with the time we had. From climbing up trailheads to hitting the local shops, we had been trying to suck the most we could out of this week. But something was different this morning.

Maybe it was the time of day—very early. The air was as clear as could be, the water was still, and the wind was calm. The forest was silent, with no rush of wind to ruffle the treetops. Maybe it was the kids becoming more attuned to the beauty and magnificence of this place. A quiet understanding was growing among them. This trip, this place, this shared experience was something special. Maybe they were able to sense that this might be a once-in-a-lifetime chance, and they were not going to waste it or take it lightly.

Today was a last-minute, impulse hike. I had seen the trail signs when we stopped near Num-Ti-Jah Lodge and plundered its gift shop on our way back from Jasper to Lake Louise. I'd noticed those signs at least half a dozen times before. But this time, when I saw the sign for the Bow Glacier Falls hike, it looked like exactly what we needed to explore as a family. I knew this waterfall hike would be incredible, and I really wanted my kids to enjoy it. Plus it would give them some extra uphill hiking practice on a modest trail before Kevin and I took them on the tougher Agnes Lake hike later in the week.

The Bow Falls trail was considered "moderate" in exertion, which in Canadian talk means it will kick an American's behind. The sign said it was about six miles round-trip, fairly steep, and ended at the mouth of the valley where the glacier slid over the lip of the mountain peak. From there the spring snowmelt drained its pure, icy water into a hundred-meter plunge to the riverbed that fed Bow Lake. These falls were the source of that wonderful lake, and they had to be discovered. As we started out, we could see the falls cascading off in the distance, roughly three miles away, but they were far enough to be difficult to focus on with the naked eye.

We crested the trail after a few hours, arriving at a rock-strewn, glacial moraine. Trickling streams and creeks crisscrossed the base of the hundred-meter falls like the arms of a giant octopus. The rock was dark, almost gray, and the water made it darker still when wet. The spray from the falls was much greater and the volume of snow-melt much higher than it had seemed from the overlook three miles back. The river crashed down a series of stair-stepping rock ledges that could easily be climbed. So we did.

We climbed around and under Bow Glacier Falls, exploring the valley for at least an hour, gorging on the sunlight, serenity, and phenomenally beautiful view. We looked back to the bluest of blue lakes below and the rustic Num-Ti-Jah Lodge in the distance. The only highway was a slender black ribbon far below, where the cars and tourist buses were mere specks on the side of the lakeshore. We were up with the eagles now, as high as we could climb without technical gear to aid our ascent.

The kids had formed a little *inuksuk*—an ancient stone marker created by the Inuit people that was often used for navigation, a point of reference, or a marker for travel routes. A Canadian symbol of the people, this design was used as the national emblem for Canada at the Vancouver Winter Olympics in 2010. The kids built theirs about two feet high out of mountain rock, picking just the right pieces out of the millions of loose shale and rock fragments that covered the ground at the base of this wonderful hideaway. They were busy climbing, exploring, taking pictures, posing in the sunlight, and picking alpine flowers for their journals. They sang, laughed, and soaked up this remarkable life moment like sponges.

I had climbed up as far as possible on the falls' ledges to look out for bears or other threats below. As I watched from above, I had the sense that something significant was occurring in the lives of my three kids and my nieces and nephew. Somehow, in the power of this pure and pristine wilderness moment, God was calling to their hearts, wooing them to come, see, and follow after him. Not because their parents did or because they would feel guilty if they didn't, but out of the sheer pleasure of being in his presence . . . like the moment they were sharing now on the top of this mountain.

Paige, Judy, and my mom met us around lunchtime at the trailhead on Bow Lake to have coffee and lunch at the lodge. The excited babble of eight people trying to talk at the same time was all anyone could hear for half an hour after we reunited. Something unusually cool had just happened. It was like a transfer of life—a sensation that the same love I had for the beauty of this place, combined with a deep passion for Christ, had somehow been implanted in the hearts of my kids. They hadn't magically "absorbed" my love for nature or my faith in God; they had experienced his glory for themselves. I shared that sensation with my wife that evening in our little loft area and tried to express how special it had been. The pictures on our cameras, the stories of the kids downstairs—still talking and laughing about what they had seen and how sore their legs were after the long hike—were all around us. The weight of the event was almost tangible to us both as we discussed how this might have been a key moment in our kids' lives.

Our trail time formed a powerful realization for me, one that carried the momentum of this book's genesis from concept to reality: Our physical hike, from the early morning roadside overlook trail to the falls where we ended, was nearly identical to the spiritual process of getting to know God personally. Let me unpack that idea just a bit.

Going Deeper with Our Hike

Many churched kids or "cultural Christians" have decent knowledge about God, but they have not met him personally. It's like students who take a class in political science. They study the US presidents to the point of becoming experts, yet they never think of them as real people. They have a basic understanding of where the presidents came from, as well as their accomplishments, failures, and history, but they have no idea about each one's personality or character. They memorize all the pertinent facts—date and place of birth, full name, parents, education, accomplishments, and contributions to society—but they never get to touch or sense the objects they are studying so carefully. Consumed by factual details, they have missed the greater part of the whole. They have a strong understanding of the topic but lack the personal relationship to be changed by what they've learned.

The same is true for many Christian students, whether kids or adults. We study God, learn about his teachings, read his book, and say his prayer, but in the end we never invite him over. We fail to meet him one-on-one, and in doing so, we miss the entire point. As parents and pastors, we may be in danger of raising a generation of well-educated students of Christ who have no idea who it is they are studying and what he really offers.

So to get back to my trail illustration, let's say the object of your study is Bow Falls. If you stop by the Bow Falls overlook, you can take beautiful pictures of the falls, read the informational signs about its creation, formation, flow, and depth . . . and mark one more accomplishment off your study list and move on to the next one without any regrets. You would be correct in saying that you have been to Bow Falls, and it was great. You could even say you are knowledgeable about it, much more so than, say, those who have never even been to Canada.

However, piling off a forty-passenger tour bus for ten minutes to snap pictures and grab a brochure is not the same as taking a day hike up to the glacier itself. Both groups of people could claim honestly that they have been to Bow Falls. But only one of those groups could say that they *know* Bow Falls. Those who hiked the trail have touched it, smelled it, climbed it, and immersed themselves in its beauty.

Such is the nature of God to our kids. Too often they see him as "there," somewhere off in the distance, beautiful yet removed from their lives. They took the church tour bus their parents made them ride, and when it stopped at the right overlook, they got out with everyone else and dutifully took the pictures, read the brochures, and bought the T-shirt. But when they came back from the tour, they didn't have a clue what it meant. They didn't experience any deep changes or transformation as a result of their visit. Following Christ has not become a reality for them, and until it does, it's only a hollow shell of a true relationship—a sterile, distant observance, a vague belief—which is a far cry from genuine faith.

I believe God is asking us as parents and families to get out of the bus and put on our hiking boots. He wants us to grab a backpack, a warm jacket, and some water and prepare to exert ourselves, sacrificing our time, energy, and resources to follow him wherever he leads us. I don't know where that will be for everyone, but I do know the route will resemble the trail we took to Bow Falls.

It will be beautiful, dangerous, and unpredictable. It will be steep and flat, high and low, dry and wet, narrow at times and wide as a meadow at others. The trail may force us to walk single file or in a bunch. It may require us to reach up and grab the hands of those ahead of us for assistance, and later we might have to reach back to help those behind us. It will reveal spectacular panoramic vistas of where we've been and give us glimpses through the trees of where we are going. Sometimes our route will put us in a narrow slit in the rock wall, as we slide through an opening barely wide enough for us to breathe. We will encounter days of great weather and sunny skies, and at other times we'll endure the discomfort and disorientation of rain, fog, sleet, or snow. As we hike this trail, I believe we all will grow. We'll each gain a greater appreciation for the awesome forces involved in our lives. As we travel the path ahead, we'll be reminded of the existence of wild and untamed life, as well as the beauty of untainted Creation. This difficult trail forces us to acknowledge our frailty and our absolute dependence on God for sustenance, protection, and safety. I think you get the idea. Nothing can replace the personal journey of faith that comes from choosing to walk out our relationship with God one-on-one.

Transformation

This truth seems to be especially vital for us to share with the current generation of teens, and ever more so as we see the growing crisis of faith our churches are experiencing. I believe that no shortcuts, no behavior modification, and no canned discipleship studies will help us transfer our Christian faith to our kids. If we want to guide our children from having knowledge *about* God to trusting God himself, they must see us parents and pastors surrender our hearts to the one who created us, and they must see the evidence of our radically changed lives. Without observing that authentic change in our hearts, without seeing an overflowing source of life and love fuel our homes and churches, this generation of kids won't accept our faith as genuine. And can you blame them? How can they get excited about God if our faith is mechanical and boring? We need to show them what it looks like to follow Jesus wholeheartedly. Then, just as we have, they must fall in love with God and pursue him and his beauty with heartfelt gratitude, passion, and the power of a transformed life. That requires the Holy Spirit to be present, and no one can fake that for long.

Jesus never told us it would be easy. He promised us in the Gospels that a man must be transformed, "born anew" to follow him into his Kingdom. Our casual discussion of being "born again" is cliché to our kids, but what it's meant to describe is a total change, a metamorphosis. Our faith should rearrange our lives entirely, until we are as different from our old selves as a caterpillar is from a butterfly. Our kids are quick to ask Jesus into their hearts, to seek out the "born again" rite of passage we all have grown so familiar with. They might have an emotional experience at a summer camp or on a retreat; sometimes it's a moving Christian concert or a special outreach geared for youth. But most of those prayers are simply an expression of our desire to gain some fire insurance, if you will. We want Jesus to be our Savior so we can go to heaven when we die, not because we actually want to surrender ourselves to him. Our faith becomes little more than a convenient painkiller. We begin to use God like we do a bottle of Advil. When life hurts, we take a dose of religion or reconnect with church to relieve our suffering temporarily, but it rarely sticks with us. That kind of faith rarely transforms our lives.

For us or our kids to make the critical second step of faith—that of asking God to be our Lord—it's going to take a lot more than just fear-based living. It's going to take our surrendering our wills to his, completely and totally. From that surrender will bloom a willingness to follow Jesus wherever he leads. Immediately we will notice peace and comfort in our lives, a new presence in our minds and hearts. From that presence will flow a love that doesn't rely on our feelings to exist. This love will grow and grow, and in the process, it will offset our natural fears and our desire to please only ourselves. But it takes real, soul-deep surrender to experience this kind of transformation and relationship with God.

This new love and trust in God cannot be adequately explained or described. No two transformations are alike. Like the beauty of a sunrise, each one is unique. But the key is that all this newness will create a desire to give up what we think we want for what God says is going to be better. It won't be fear or guilt or shame that forces us to control our behaviors. We will voluntarily submit ourselves to him, with genuine gratitude and an understanding of God's place in our world.

Can we all agree that a surrendered life does indeed impact our world? We and our kids can be transformed—but as parents, we must go first. Only someone who has been personally transformed by Jesus can successfully lead another life on the same path to intimacy. Jesus called it being a disciple, and this marks the follower of Christ with a profoundly different view of life and of the world. It's a view that cannot be forced or memorized. It must first be felt, then believed in, and ultimately relied upon.

Going Forward

No matter how strong our faith is, it will not automatically be passed down to the next generation. Our children must encounter the living God for themselves! Nothing else will transform their minds and hearts. On the trail to Bow Falls, my kids began to experience God in a new, personal way. And I didn't have to say a word. God did take my hand and lead me to the right time and place to make sure they didn't miss it, but in the end it was his power and his Spirit that changed the condition of their hearts—not me, not our church.

It took a crisis in my daughter's life to get my attention, to convince me to make my kids the top priority in my life after God and my wife. I had to admit how little I really knew about God myself and how weak my faith was. I had to be willing to take my own personal hike up the proverbial mountainside before I could lead others to follow. Just reading the guidebook and sending them off and on their way is not going to work. We have to go there ourselves first and then come back for our kids to have any hope of changing their hearts.

This is the revelation I gained in my hike that day. God showed it to me when I wasn't even looking, just like he said he would. If you seek him on your journey, he will do something similar for you as well.

Our Family Journal Entries from Our Week in Canada

As you read this week's journal entries from Paige and my three kids, you will see that their focus and interests are much different. They were enjoying many new experiences and learning to be supportive and encouraging of each other along the way. They were reconnecting as siblings, and I was reconnecting as their father. Paige and I also grew closer as husband and wife. By the time we left, we were a stronger, tighter family unit.

Including these journal notes and personal perspectives is not meant to be a selfish "proud papa" moment for me to brag about my family. Instead, it's meant to show the normality of our kids and their reactions to the trip. Reading this all just from my perspective, the reader might be tempted to think our kids were all suddenly ready for the Rapture after spending a day on a hike in Canada. Not so much. These journal entries prove that some of the trip was amazing, and some of it was not. The words my kids wrote accurately reflect what happened and should bring encouragement to those who feel as if their version of life is only in plain old vanilla flavor. And maybe these journal entries will encourage you to pursue a similar experience with your family.

June 22, 2010—Tuesday

CALEB—*The first day in Canada was really fun! I was happy to sleep in. I remember the first thing I bought when we went to the gift shop (Moraine Lake) was a thermostat magnet. Then we went to Bow Lake, and I LOVED IT! (My favorite lake) Then Peyto Lake, which I thought was the prettiest lake in Canada. It was fun going up and playing with snow. We also had a snowball fight. Suzanna and I were trying to get Colleen and Bethany when BAM! a stranger hit Suzanna with a snowball. Then the stranger's wife said we could hit him back so we did and almost hit him right on the head, but he ducked. Then we saw some robin's eggs in a nest by our cabin. I thought it was AWESOME!*

BETHANY—*Our first day in Canada was great! We went to Moraine Lake gift shop. Later we went to Peyto Lake and hiked to the top. My favorite part of the day was the snowball fight between our cousins, Caleb, and Dad. Caleb and Dad wiped out (fell). It was fantastic!*

JESSICA—*I was ON this day because it was our first day to explore Canada! I loved hiking out to Peyto Lake because the view was amazing! There were a ton of tourists there, and it was funny because we got our picture taken by people from the Netherlands, and at the same time we heard a British family talking about their trip. I loved seeing all the different cultures, even the tons of Japanese bus tourists. Bow Lake was really cool too because the water was so clear! Oh, and I loved the Takakkaw Falls because Mom and I discovered a marmot! It was a cool day! Canada met my expectations! It was great!*

PAIGE—*Today was our first full day in Canada. Brad and Uncle Kevin hiked the Plain of Six Glaciers to the teahouse. The rest of* us went to Moraine Lake and shopped in the gift shop. It was cold and rainy there. We met back up with the guys at the cabin and then all went to Bow Lake, hiked to Peyto Lake, and then went to see Takakkaw Falls. This day I noticed a robin's nest in the small Douglas fir tree in front of our cabin. It had 3 eggs in it. We ate chicken alfredo pasta in the cabin that evening.

June 23, 2010—Wednesday

CALEB—*Definitely my favorite hike and my favorite day. The hike was so pretty, and we made inuksuks out of stones at the end. The glacier was cool (no pun intended), and I got glacier water! So much better than non-glacier water. Then we went shopping, and I got a kinder egg which was AWESOME-SAUCE! It had a chicken with dice in it. My new favorite candy thing (kinder eggs). Then Lake Louise was cool but not my favorite.*

BETHANY—*Great day. We hiked at 6:00 a.m. to a waterfall at Bow Lake. The hike up was tiring and strenuous, but the beautiful falls and unforgettable views made it worth the while. Oh, and we met a wonderful British man. He was quite fantastic. Later we went to the glacier (Athabasca). It was really fun, but I did get a little nervous when standing on the ice. Before heading back to the cabin we stopped at a shopping mall! Colleen and I discovered some seriously amazing chips! In the candy store we bought out the German chocolate eggs called Kinder Surprises! They had a double layer of chocolate and a toy inside.*

JESSICA—*This hike (Bow Falls) was amazing. I loved how first we were on a trail in the woods, then it turned into a valley of rocks, and then the terrain just kept on changing! It was beautiful; the day just kept getting better because we got to walk on a glacier! The ride* *there was a little freaky because the machines go down this huge incline and you feel like you're gonna tip over. The glacier was cool to walk on top of. We also saw a Sun Dog, and that was cool. I'd never even heard of one before! So that was a pretty sweet day!*

PAIGE—*The crew woke up early today to hike the Bow Lake Falls trail. Mimi, Aunt Judy, and I slept in and met up with everyone later at Num-Ti-Jah Lodge on Bow Lake. Then we all headed to the Athabasca Glacier. We ate lunch at the very pricey visitor's center cafeteria, and then we headed to our tour out on the glacier. We rode in a specialized snow coach. The kids were able to fill up bottles with glacier water! Heading back to Lake Louise we stopped at Saskatchewan Crossing to shop a bit. We also stopped at Lake Louise shops. FUN! That night we ate lasagna in the cabin.*

June 24, 2010—Thursday

CALEB—*Jasper (the town) was neat, but it was too old for me. I got a lot of stuff there though. Athabasca Falls was very cool, my favorite waterfall. All the animals we saw were amazing, as we got so close. The highlight of my day was seeing the eggs hatching in the robin's nest, because I love animals. They (baby birds) looked like silly putty. Pretty nasty.*

BETHANY—*Well, the shopping in Jasper was awesome! We had a nice lunch at Smitty's (restaurant). Although we didn't end up going on the boat ride (Maligne Lake), I enjoyed seeing the lake. We saw a lot of wildlife on the way, and when we came home to the cabins, the eggs had hatched. Cool to see!*

JESSICA—*This day was pretty fun. We got a lot of good shopping in at Jasper, and I found some great stuff! I was really disappointed* *when we couldn't go on the boat ride (Maligne Lake) due to weather though.*

PAIGE—*We all got up at 6:00 a.m. (except Mimi and Woolie) and headed north to Jasper, about 3 hours away from our cabins. On the way we stopped at Athabasca Falls. In Jasper we ate lunch and shopped. We really liked the "Friends of Jasper" store. Unfortunately the day was rainy so we didn't get to go out on the Maligne Lake boat tour. Brad had wanted to take us up to Mt. Edith Cavell, but it was closed for road repairs. Disappointment! However, back in Jasper we found a really good pizza place and saw lots of really cool animals that day. Elk, black bear, weasel, bighorn sheep, mule deer, mountain goats, and a caribou. It was a long ride back to the Chalets. Arrived at 10:30, and the robin's eggs had hatched in their nest.*

June 25, 2010—Friday

CALEB—*It was so cold at Lake Louise, but the food was delicious. The waiter we had was funny too. At the hotel I got some ice cream and kinder eggs. I really, really, really, really, really, really liked Banff. It was so cool, then the Old Spaghetti Factory was amazing. Except the lemonade they served had like rosemary in it. Eww, yuck. Then I was disappointed the third egg had not hatched when we got back to the cabins. Pretty mellow day.*

BETHANY—*Lunch at Lake Louise was GREAT! I had a really yummy pizza, and I successfully convinced some dudes that I was British! VICTORY! Then we went shopping in Banff. I got shorts and an awesomely cool ROXY hat at the Quicksilver store. We went to dinner at the Old Spaghetti Factory, which was fun. Good day!*

JESSICA—*Shopping in Banff was really cool. They have a ton of shops, and Suzanna and I were on our search for the "perfect hoodie"! I also loved the spaghetti factory. It was sooo good! Pretty fun day!*

PAIGE—*Brad and Kevin hiked at Lake Louise again on the small and big beehive trails. The rest of us met up with them for lunch at Lake Louise hotel. Afterwards, everyone except me went to Banff to shop and have dinner. They ate at the Old Spaghetti Factory. I stayed at the cabin and rested, then spent time down by Bakers Creek—next to our cabins.*

June 26, 2010—Saturday
Caleb, Bethany, and Jessica didn't contribute to the journal for our week in Canada past Friday the 25th. (It appears the kids were exhausted from so much hiking, shopping, and late-night playing in the cabins. A good problem to have.)

PAIGE—*Our last full day in Canada! All of us except Mimi and Woolie hiked the teahouse trail at Lake Louise. At the end was beautiful Lake Agnes and the teahouse. We all had sandwiches and tea. Then we hiked to the end of the lake and played on rocks and built inuksuks out of stones. AWESOME morning! Then it was off to Emerald Lake for lunch with Mimi and Woolie. We saw a grizzly bear on the roadside. Spent the evening in Banff.* ☺

TEN

CANADA TO YELLOWSTONE AND A MEMORY IN THE TETONS

The world is a book, and those who do not travel read only one page.

ST. AUGUSTINE OF HIPPO

Sunday, June 27, 2010

Our week in Canada was extraordinary. Not because we had planned it out so well, or because we did all the expensive and cool tourist things, but because the hand of God was on us. I could sense his pleasure at our efforts to draw near to his masterpiece we call the Canadian Rockies. I could feel his favor helping us grow together and experience the beauty of his Creation as it was meant to be. I could tell my kids were beginning to sense this blessing too.

As we moved into the second week of the trip, there were no more heated car fights or "he said/she said" back-and-forth battles. Gone were the bitingly sarcastic remarks and the "Get out of my space, or I'm gonna hurt you" verbal spats. Absent were the bored, comatose looks in my rearview mirror. My subdued, emotionally distant teenagers were coming alive again. I could feel it. They were reawakening to the joy of discovery, to the childlike thrill of experiencing new things and learning about different places, peoples, and cultures.

As my kids began to sense the enormity of the trip—the epic stage of the iconic West and the majesty of the mountains, lakes, and forests—they, on their own initiative, began to set down their technologies and unplug from the safety of all that was familiar and distracting. I believe they sensed the power of the beauty around them to inspire, uplift, and redirect their dreams to something bigger than themselves. The result was that less iPod and more "i-talk" was occurring in the car. We were discussing the history, culture, and weather of the areas we drove through and looking for historical signs and interesting landmarks to stop and check out. They wanted me to pull the car over at scenic vistas and roadside rest areas. Their focus was subtly shifting from entertaining themselves to discovering more about the world around them.

I wouldn't have asked for anything else from this trip, but God had more in store for each of us in the days ahead. After my parents flew home, we had planned to drive south out of Lake Louise and Banff into Waterton National Park on the Canadian side of the border and then into Glacier National Park on the US side.

We took back roads (open only in summer) down the edge of the Continental Divide to Waterton and skipped the congestion around one of Canada's largest cities, Calgary. The road we chose was two-lane, twisty, and beautiful to drive on. The kids seemed eager to move into the next week of our trip. We had battled cold, wind, and rain for three of the six days we had been in Canada, and the warmer, sunnier climate of the northern US was calling.

On the way we got hit by a flu bug—or rather, Jessica did. We had just finished a two-hour cruise and sightseeing tour across the border from Waterton to Glacier National Park. On the cruise we were enjoying an incredibly beautiful sunset over the still lake and mountains when Jessica suddenly was not feeling her best. Jessica is our oldest and most mature child, so if she was in pain and telling us about it on a family vacation, we knew it was bad. Instead of trying to drive on in the dusk to cross the border back into the States, we looked for a hotel where she could rest and recuperate for the evening.

We finally found one. An old, dingy motel that had seen better years, it looked like it had been framed in the late thirties or early forties and had never been updated. It was in a distinct state of disrepair and offered only fifteen rooms. Ours was outfitted with mismatched furniture, including an old black-and-white, six-channel, twelve-inch-screen TV on a rickety table. The rooms carried a musty retirement-home smell. If you were optimistic, you could say it had a very retro vibe. No air-conditioning, no screens on the windows, a threadbare sofa crowded out by an ancient queen bed that almost filled the main room, and a pair of twin mattresses in the tiny, wood-panel-encrusted second room. The bathroom was closet-size, with a small sink, toilet, and walk-in tile shower. Things would be pretty cramped for the five of us, but we had no choice. Jessica was feeling worse by the moment, and this popular tourist town was booked solid. In minutes Jessica's discomfort had moved from unease to a full-on raging flu extravaganza.

I think she might have slept an hour total that night, and I was up with her the whole way. I know, usually moms do that sort of thing, but that night I felt like it was supposed to be me. As she thrashed in her tiny twin bed, I dutifully stayed up, rubbing her back and neck and shoulders, getting her the last orange Gatorade from our SUV to keep her hydrated. Crackers, ginger ale—whatever she wanted or needed, I got it. I whispered to her, I soothed her, and when she was repeatedly sick, I sat up with her until she slowly relaxed on the old sagging mattress. I watched carefully as she fell fitfully asleep for a few minutes. When the next wave of nausea hit, we would start the whole cycle all over again. She was miserable.

As I sat in the darkness with her in this beat-up, smelly hotel, I realized how much I loved her. She was always going to be my little girl, but she had really grown up this year. She was going to be a junior in high school already! She had her driver's license now and would soon be going off to college. All in the blink of an eye. It wasn't a bad thing, but it was a sad recognition for me of how fast the time had passed—and of how often I had focused on her sister's or brother's issues rather than on Jessica's. She was always the good kid, never needed much discipline or correction, and just instinctively seemed to make wise choices. So, not being the squeaky wheel, she didn't get much grease, or in our case, attention.

Tonight, I was determined to give her the grease, so to speak. She was the focus of all my attention, love, and support. Just her; no one else mattered as much that night. I suffered along with her in the pain and the waves of nausea that gripped her every forty-five minutes all night long, and when she came out from the bathroom, yellow with sickness, I wiped her feverish forehead with the only cool and clean cloth in the place. It was my honor to do so. To serve her, to protect her, to show her with my actions and my efforts that nothing could prevent me from loving her, from holding her, from being her dad—not sickness, not our odd location, and most certainly not her nearing adulthood.

I don't know if she ever understood all that I felt that night.

Fortunately, the virus or food poisoning or whatever had attacked her slowly faded in the next twenty-four hours. As we drove up and over the Glacier National Park passes the next morning, with dozens of feet of snowpack still visible, I was watching my "little" girl in the rearview mirror. Anxious to confirm that she was indeed improving, I barely noticed the mountainous terrain and natural beauty around us.

I'm not bragging here. Jessica was the real trouper, battling through her sickness like she did. I'm only sharing this story to honor my oldest child with my profound appreciation. I want to give my written testament of the love and respect Paige and I have for the wonderful young woman she has grown to be. I also want to remind other parents to keep a careful eye on their "well-adjusted" children, not to neglect them or assume they don't need your help. Their more-challenging siblings might require extra time and attention, but remember that all of your children need you, each in their own way.

Jessica was always the low-maintenance daughter. Quick to respond to our direction and careful to be respectful and encouraging to others, she was so easy to parent that we often took her for granted. It was easy to focus most of our energy on her younger sister and brother. I wish I had taken more time to tell her how much I admired how she endured the difficulties of her siblings without complaint. If time would allow, I would go back and take her on more daddy-daughter dates to show her she was loved every bit as much as Bethany and Caleb. Far too often I allowed last-minute interruptions and family drama to disrupt our planned outings, and that's an issue I still regret. But in the end Paige and I did our best to put out the fires and carry on.

This book itself could be misconstrued as another over-focused parenting reaction to our middle child, at the expense of our other two kids. It is not. This book and our road trip were for our whole family. Bethany's experience was just a catalyst for change—first in me, then in all of us. God used Bethany's crisis to rearrange our home priorities and values, bringing them back into alignment with his.

Monday, June 28, 2010

After surviving a night with the flu, Jessica slept for most of the day in the SUV. She missed the crossing over the snow-filled glacier pass and the Glacier National Park visitor's center. She missed the descent into Montana's flathead country and the winding, never-ending Highway 83 as it snaked its way south out of Kalispell to our next destination: Yellowstone! The countryside changed as we descended out of the cloud-tipped peaks of Glacier Park and back into the fertile and warmer lower elevations of the Montana countryside.

Traffic here was nonexistent. We were out of the main tourist channels and back into the two-lane world. After the nonstop hustle and hurry of Banff, it was a welcome relief to be able to watch the valleys and tree-covered foothills roll by while the scent of evergreen tree sap filled the air. It was so peaceful. The kids and Paige were chilling, and I was drooping a bit. Between my lack of sleep the night before and now the warmer, sun-filled skies, I was beyond relaxed. My body felt like it was made of putty. I stuck with my self-appointed role as the driver, but I was in need of some coffee or Coke or something to keep my eyelids open.

The drive from Glacier Park south seemed to take at least two days instead of half of one, thanks to the reduced speed limit and winding road we took to I-90. If the kids hadn't been so tired, I'm confident we would have endured an epidemic of car sickness from the drive. A full-size SUV is not the best vehicle for hugging tight curves; although it's a very capable family hauler, a go-kart it is not. I struggled to keep the speeds slow enough to not wake my peaceful and precious cargo.

We finally made it to Butte, Montana, and a very pricey Holiday Inn Express in the middle of nowhere. Butte was an Old West town right out of the movies, full of ranchers, miners, cowboys, and semi-trucks. But we were weary, and it was clean. So we paid and enjoyed our brief respite from the road.

Tuesday, June 29, 2010—Paige's Birthday in Yellowstone

The next day we were up and at it, healthy, refreshed, and well fed. We were heading for West Yellowstone, Montana, to get a decent hotel. We planned to spend at least two and half days exploring the first and most popular national park in our nation. I had never visited the park in the summertime as an adult, and I was anxious to see if it was as awesome as the critics said. The kids didn't know what to expect, but they had been bitten by the exploring bug and were eagerly reviewing their park maps and tourist attraction brochures. The weather continued to warm and clear the farther south we went, and by late morning we were in West Yellowstone.

Paige thought we had forgotten it was her forty-second birthday, but we had not. We surprised her with a late birthday breakfast at a great pancake house in West Yellowstone near our hotel. They brought out the neatest pancake—a special treat for birthdays, complete with brightly colored candles and a song. Since my parents had flown back to Nashville after Lake Louise, our group now was reduced to just my brother's family and ours, but we still needed a large dining table for all ten of us to sit together. It was great to see our little gang celebrating and laughing and connecting again after the hours we had been apart on the road. Like a scene from an old movie, we were in a Western-style room with long wooden tables, our six laughing, excited teens sharing a family meal with their parents. It was as if on our trip we had formed a renewed bond of love, acceptance, and pride in each other.

I knew that God was up to more than just reconnecting me with my kids. He was active with my brother, my sister-in-law, and their children too. My nieces, Suzanna and Colleen, were identical twins. Having just graduated high school mere weeks before, they were preparing to leave for their first year of college at the end of the summer. This was a critical time for them, a transition from young adult to full-on adult. I could see the tension in my brother's eyes and feel his fear and sadness. Would they be okay? Had he done enough to reach their hearts, or would their beliefs fade among the lure of the new freedoms and lifestyle options available on a college campus? He was concerned, but I sensed he was also very grateful for the two weeks they had on this trip to connect and reaffirm their love as a family.

Yellowstone is every bit as amazing as Banff. No doubt the time we had to enjoy it was a mere fraction of what is needed to fully explore the beauty of the area. It's vast, enormous, gigantic—no adjective seems to capture its true size. The largest of our national parks, it covers hundreds of square miles and feels more like a whole state than a wilderness park. Its roads, hotels, lodges, and restaurants are well organized and efficient, and the hundreds of fascinating sights, sounds, and smells came too frequently for us to stop and enjoy every one. But we did our best, stopping at dozens of boardwalks to see geysers, sulfur pits, tar pits, bubbling volcanic mudpots, steaming mud flats, acid ponds, buffalo (bison, technically), grizzly bears, wolves, elk, deer, mountain lions, eagles. You name it, they live in Yellowstone. Wild, rugged, and yet accessible by car, it's a fantastic blend of modern and protected. I loved it. Paige and the kids did too.

We made it to most if not all of the iconic photo op locales—the Grand Falls overlook, Old Faithful, the historic wooden lodge that Teddy Roosevelt built, the Grand Lake, and many mountain passes. We stopped at the grand old hotels and turn-of-the-century gift shops, all beautifully maintained and equipped for millions of annual tourists to discover. Everything was exceptionally cool and more beautiful than any description I can share here. If you haven't gone to Yellowstone before, my advice is to make it happen. It's worth the effort.

Meanwhile, something was going on with my brother. I sensed that this portion of the trip, more than any other, was prepared by God for him. While Yellowstone was great, it wasn't holding Kevin's attention. Whenever we opened the maps or took a break at an overlook, he was always looking south—and eventually I realized he was hoping to see the Grand Tetons just a few miles south of Yellowstone. We talked about the possibility of making a quick visit since we were already out here and it was less than an hour away. When I offered to go, he took me up on it in a heartbeat.

Time was short, as our families were going to have to separate on the way back home. His clan was leaving the West; they had to return back east through Chicago and then on to North Carolina. My family would be staying in the mountains for several more days, heading south to Colorado and then Santa Fe before returning home to Tennessee. Grand Teton National Park was on the way for us and out of the way for Kevin—but he really wanted to see it before they had to leave. So we did.

Wednesday, June 30, 2010—Teton National Park and Kevin's Special Day

On our second day at Yellowstone, we loaded up to drive south to see the Tetons. When we made it to the Grand Targhee Lodge, the splendor of the view astounded us. A panorama of natural beauty surrounded us. The mountains in Grand Teton National Park are unique, with jagged projections of knifelike peaks stabbing their way into the blue sky. The lodge itself was built on a valley floor overlooking a lake about three or four miles from the highest of the peaks—named Grand Teton, of course. There we had a full lunch and felt like kings and queens at a banquet. The dining room had plenty of elegant, old Western charm, with high wooden ceilings, crystal chandeliers, and even a wall of glass so we could take in the magnificent views while we ate.

The food was superb, and I could tell my brother absolutely loved this place. I couldn't quite figure out the depth of his emotion. I knew some people were major fans because of Ansel Adams's famous black-and-white photographs of the area, but the majority of summer tourists stuck mostly to Yellowstone for a reason. Sure, the Grand Teton view was amazing, but not any more so than the hundreds of places we had just seen in the Canadian Rockies, Glacier Park, or Yellowstone. What was so special about Teton?

The answer came in the lodge's gift store. My brother picked out a sixties-era postcard/poster print of the original lodge that triggered in him an old memory of being here as a little boy. Before I was hatched, Mom and Dad had taken Kevin out here for a fun summer vacation. This would have been in the early to mid-1960s, before the big-money ski developments and crazy tourist attractions in Jackson Hole and Yellowstone were created. Everything was different now, with new buildings and new attractions, and Kevin hadn't realized until that moment that this was the same place where he had stayed as a boy. He spoke wistfully of riding on a horse with our dad, having a cowboy chuckwagon supper somewhere up on the mountain, and spending a few days alone with Dad in the old Western town of Jackson Hole, Wyoming. A piece of his childhood had been hidden there in that Grand Teton gift shop, and he was rediscovering it for himself and sharing it with his now-grown kids and wife right in front of me. It was special and intimate, and it created a shared memory they could carry forward together as a family.

My brother is not an overly outgoing, warm-and-fuzzy type of fellow; he is a strong, responsible, straight-talking, confident, and commanding typical older brother who believes he is always right (which he usually is) and generally barks out facts in conversations more than he talks. But he has a soft and gentle heart, loyal and loving to the core, so his bark is much worse than his bite. His kids would say he has a firm style of fathering and a black-and-white way of viewing the world. He is often misinterpreted as stern or angry, when in fact he is just focused, confident, and intense in his personal opinions and beliefs. (I share some of these traits as well.) But at this moment, he was misty-eyed and gentle as a puppy as he shared about the time he had spent here long ago when he was a little boy of six or seven, wide-eyed and awed to be a part of the old Wild West.

When he was last in Teton, he had been a child. Today, as a fifty-year-old man, he was again open and vulnerable as he talked to us all about his childhood and his memories of being with our dad in this very spot over forty years ago. He could see suddenly how quickly time was racing by, and I could tell how much he wanted to slow things down so he could do just a little more with his kids before they grew up completely and left home for good. I could identify with his sadness, his longing, his pain. I was only two years behind him with my own kids, and I wasn't looking forward to that transition at all.

This morning we all had seen a side of my brother that had been hidden, and now I understood why it had been important for them to make it to Teton before heading east the next morning. This was an important place, and God wanted my brother to rediscover this part of his childhood before the chance to share it with his kids was lost forever.

The situation helped me to understand my brother better. I'm younger by nine years and had grown up idolizing Kevin. He was smarter, stronger, and faster than I was. He seemed invincible. Yet in this moment I saw past the many seemingly strong facets of his personality to the little boy that still remained, and I understood how fragile and sweet and good his soul was. It was like God allowed me to have a front-row seat to see how he orchestrates the moments of our lives to be beautiful and precious in ways that we could never have hoped to see on our own. I was feeling the father-heart of God to his children, experiencing firsthand the gentle way he cares for our hurts and fears and failings.

This moment helped me (and, I'm sure, my brother) become more aware of how important this memory could be for our kids someday. Maybe one distant day they will return with their own children and reflect on this trip and how special it was for them—a tradition passed on from one generation of Mathiases to another.

We all bought some trinkets and memorabilia and headed back up to West Yellowstone. As we piled into our cars, we knew it would be our last time together as an extended family on this trip. We were grateful for the chance to have one more meaningful night together in the huge and beautiful park, but we were all a bit saddened to realize that our journey was about to go in different directions. Despite that, I was fully relaxed, knowing that life was indeed as it should be. I felt a great peace settle over our family that night, and I had a sense of something deep within my brother that had been reconciled. It was a closing of the distant past and a sad but honest turning forward into the future, a movement from regret to anticipation—something I'm sure I will find out for myself in the very near future, when my own kids reach the milestones of adulthood.

I believe that God was using our time together on this trip to help each of us grow, heal, and renew ourselves, both with him and with each other. He had prepared these two weeks for our good, to bless us and to restore us. The pain and frustrations of the recent months had started to rob us of our purpose, our confidence, and the joy of simply living. My sister-in-law, Judy, had almost died eight months before of a sudden stroke, only to recover and successfully join us on the Agnes Lake trail in Banff. Judy had been triumphant in her extraordinary effort to make it all the way up one of the toughest trails we did that week. My dad had suffered a heart attack less than a year before and had narrowly survived quadruple-bypass surgery. More than ever, we were all acutely aware of the frailty and uncertainty of life. We knew each time we gathered together as an extended family was a gift, and we were grateful for the chance to be with each other and see what God had been doing in all of our lives.

A Grander Purpose

This trip began to represent a whole lot more than just a personal recovery for Bethany and my immediate family. My myopic vision of this trip had faded in my growing awareness of the personal needs of my entire extended family, and I began to see that this trip might have been ordained by God for them as well. It seemed our trek was perfectly designed to match his prescribed will for each of our lives, and just by being obedient to take the risk, I had allowed myself and many others to be blessed.

A. W. Tozer wrote,

> An infinite God can give all of Himself to each of His children. He does not distribute Himself that each may have a part, but to each one He gives all of Himself as fully as if there were no others.[8]

I was humbled to begin to see the enormous scope and specificity of God's design—not only the way he directed us all personally, but also the intricate way he wove our paths together to become something much more beautiful. Our family was developing a powerful synergy; the whole was much greater than the sum of the individual parts. Together we formed something beyond what any of us would ever be on our own.

I was growing in my awareness of how much one single act by an individual could become a catalyst of change for us all. I was starting to realize that when I trusted God enough to simply obey, even with my limited understanding, he could then act in ways that would astonish me.

We need to grasp how critical it is for parents—and fathers, in particular—to stay close to Jesus, to spend time with him regularly and read his Word. We must be attuned to his leading and ready to follow his promptings. He will call us, and we need to be ready to answer.

I had more to learn, and God had more to reveal. But at Yellowstone and Grand Teton, I sensed the ever-present, all-powerful influence of our heavenly Father quietly working, and our response was as simple as choosing to follow his voice. Much like the words of Jesus himself as he called to the twelve disciples over two thousand years ago, I could feel him whispering to my heart: "Come, follow me."

Journal Entry:
June 27, 2010—Sunday

PAIGE—*Today we said good-bye to the Baker Creek Chalets before heading south to Waterton, Alberta. On the start to home we stopped at a laundromat in Banff—clean clothes for the journey back home! In Waterton we saw an interesting sight: Deer in* *many of the yards. They just roamed the town! We all went on a boat cruise—scenery was beautiful of course, and we crossed the dividing line between the USA and Canada on our ride on the lake. Unfortunately Jessica got very sick that night with what we think was food poisoning—a long night for her and us in our tiny hotel bathroom.* ☹

ELEVEN

LOST IN THE PRESENT AND FINDING BETHANY'S MOOSE

The gifts of the Master are these: freedom, life, hope, new direction, transformation, and intimacy with God. If the cross was the end of the story, we would have no hope. But the cross isn't the end. Jesus didn't escape from death; he conquered it and opened the way to heaven for all who will dare to believe. The truth of this moment, if we let it sweep over us, is stunning. It means Jesus really is who he claimed to be, we are really as lost as he said we are, and he really is the only way for us to intimately and spiritually connect with God again.

STEVEN JAMES, *Story*

187

Thursday, July 1, 2010

With Yellowstone now in our rearview mirror, we set off for Colorado. Before dawn we had schlepped all our travel gear back into our overstuffed Honda Pilot, delicately loading up all our new tourist treasures into the dwindling number of safe places that remained. Two large cups of McDonald's coffee, one chocolate milk, four sausage-and-cheese burritos, and an extra-large Diet Coke later, we were on our way.

To get to Colorado from West Yellowstone, you can drive either south or east out of the park. Given the time constraints and my desire to show the kids one of my favorite places (Rocky Mountain National Park), we chose to head south. That last day as we drove through the mist-shrouded landscape of Yellowstone, we saw the heads of enormous bison staring silently at our SUV as we quietly, even reverently drove past. The geysers and hot springs bubbled and gurgled as we left, unfazed by our arrival or our exit. The lake glistened in the rising dawn light, and the sky parted its clouds to show us the elegant royal blue that can be seen only at the higher elevations. It was as if the old park were giving us a fond wave farewell as we headed away to other sights, sounds, and adventures.

The roads were empty this early; the summer swarms of tourists and rental cars, buses, and RVs were yet to be seen. We had the beauty and serenity of this unrivaled vast wilderness all to ourselves as we slipped away. Everyone seemed content. We had loved each and every part of Yellowstone, from the rustic elegance of the Old Faithful Inn to the modern conveniences of its visitor centers and smooth roads. The variety of geography, wildlife, and grand vistas in Yellowstone are found nowhere else in the world, and we had experienced them as one should—with equal parts excitement, awe, and joy . . . together.

Today we would be encountering new sights and sounds (and, yes, even smells). The road ahead called us to discover its secrets. By now my entire family was thoroughly infected with wanderlust; the need to see beyond the next turn in the road was no longer just my own sickness. They were eagerly pulling out road maps and reading dozens of brochures as we planned our route south. We settled on taking Highway 287 southeast out of Teton and into the Bridger-Teton National Forest. The map showed that our chosen route would take us through remote areas. We would cross the Continental Divide west of Dubois, Wyoming, and then gradually wander south and east across a great sloping plain of high prairies and dry valleys.

We drove steadily on, fueled by our need to get back on the road and discover more and also by our growing awareness that time was running short for us to soak up as much of the beauty and atmosphere of the American West as we could. Everyone was saddened by the departure of Uncle Kevin, Aunt Judy, and the cousins, but within a few hours our focus was on the path ahead.

The Wind River Road

The Wind River Indian Reservation has been accurately named. If our vehicle had been equipped with a sail, I would have used it in a heartbeat. It would have saved at least ten miles a gallon for sure! The wind was ferocious as it scraped at the dry rock and raced us across the valleys and plains. Making the drive from west to east involved a gradual descent in altitude and followed the eastern edges of the snowcapped Wyoming Mountains. From this perspective, we could see fifty to one hundred miles at times across a vast and unsettled high prairie. Antelope, deer, elk, and bighorn sheep were there, if you took the time to look for them. The tumbleweeds were the size of garbage cans and blasted their way onto our two-lane highway,

looking like brown boulders. Most suburbanites instinctively swerve
on the road to avoid them, before they realize it's not necessary. When
hit at seventy-five miles per hour, tumbleweeds disintegrate like dust.

The roads were largely deserted. With towns of less than five
thousand people sprinkled every fifty miles or so, the area was every
bit as rural as it had looked on the map. But on the arid and vast horizon, there's an alluring beauty that's hard to describe. If you get the
chance, you really should go see it for yourself. As you drive Highway
287 eastward, you see the rugged beauty of a high-elevation prairie and even desert-like geography—vast and brown and red, with
massive flat-topped rock mesas surrounded by pockets of arroyo-like
valleys, and even green strips of grassland waterways dribbling in
from time to time. All the dry, barren, and exposed land lies to your
left, while on the right you have the exact opposite: green forests
stretching upward along the foothills, and beyond that the massive
mountaintops in the distance, twinkling as the sunlight touches
patches of snow and ice. The clouds hover over those peaks, as if an
invisible wall is holding them back, stopping them from advancing
any farther west. Eagles, hawks, and buzzards circle high above, dancing in the wind currents like lazy merry-go-rounds.

The wind was relentless as it roared at us from behind, pushing
and twisting our car forward, faster and faster. We pulled off at a
roadside overlook and looked down, across, and up at a staggering
panorama of contrasts. Mountains and valleys, greens and browns,
cold and hot, wild and serene all collided somewhere east of Dubois,
Wyoming. There was no official name, no national park—just rugged and unrestrained landscape, yet more evidence of God's artistic
desire to make things beautiful.

With serenity and perspective on one side, brokenness and dry-
ness on the other, this road is a lot like life. It's full of beauty and yet

full of suffering. We have a choice in perspectives, a choice of how we will look at the road we need to travel. Some of us look longingly at the beauty and lush provision of the mountains while we're struggling to survive a desert reality. We hate the eroded brown-and-red soil, the bone-dry ground. We hate the jagged valleys and enormous rock mesas blocking our paths. We long only for the cool breezes of the rocky heights, the smell of fresh pines and blooming flowers from forests just out of reach. It makes us crazy with frustration and resentment. We start to hate God for putting us so close to such beauty and yet so far from reaching it for ourselves.

We forget that the path we're on will at times cross over into lush and refreshing places, and we forget that it will also cross back over into the barren, rugged desert. But mostly our life paths will wind their way like this road, halfway between them both, beautiful and amazing and breathtaking in their pace and perspective. We just have to decide if we're going to look only out of the right or the left side windows.

A road trip, a vacation, a movie night with family, a date with our spouses—these are the times we have to choose to pull off the road and enjoy the view. These are opportunities to reorient ourselves, to look around at life from all sides. If we don't remember to rest and reset our vision and realities, we can become hypnotized by life's relentless pace and pressures, seeing only the things directly in front of us, oblivious to the incredible and beautiful truth of where we really are.

Caleb and Bethany could see only the mountains and lush forests, as they were on the passenger side of our SUV. Jessica, who sat directly behind me, saw only the desert and scrub brush of an elevated prairie, vast and open, a barren expanse seemingly devoid of life. In the front, Paige and I had a great view of both sides of the road and could discern the contrasting beauties of our path forward. We could anticipate the next turn in the road and understand the speed and position our vehicle would need to be in to safely navigate it.

If we had relied only on our kids for direction or input, we would have lost our way. One side was seeing and feeling one thing, while the other saw and felt something completely opposite. It took both parents in the front seat, eyes wide open, maps in hand, to correctly see the path forward for us all. It's a great illustration of the road of life we parents find ourselves navigating at home. We're often pressured to give in, to surrender what we know to be the truth of a circumstance to meet the demands and preferences of our teens.

We can't do it. We have to drive the road we know is in front of us—and trust that God will in time make the whole picture known to our kids, regardless of the current view they may have of the road. No matter what, we need to stay the course.

Lost in the Present

As we made our way southeast across central Wyoming, the mountains slowly retreated to our right and the plains began to lose their rusty desert feel. Grasslands became green, showing signs of life, and the occasional horse farm and cattle ranch began to pop up. We were moving into a more fertile land, still in the shadow of the massive mountains to the west, but seemingly a more gentle space to be in.

As we drove farther east, the road turned south, and we noticed another change. The small towns sounded as if they were named after Native Americans instead of after French or English explorers. The shift was more than historical. Sporadic ranches and farms became small groupings of old house trailers, patches of metal huts, and tiny, decades-old houses with rusted-out vehicles of every size, shape, and make spread out between them.

This was still Indian country. We were smack in the middle of a very large reservation—the Wind River Indian Reservation—and the abrupt change in the homes and villages reflected that. Poverty, it seemed, was the norm here. Homes and the lives they represented all seemed to be old and broken and worn-out. As we sped by another small town with a dilapidated gas station and a fifty-year-old brick school, we saw a single, battered, brown state roadway sign for "Sacajawea Grave Site." My daughters and wife went bananas. This was not to be missed!

I slammed on the brakes and made a U-turn back to the one intersection in the past twenty miles. A blinking yellow light hung like a lonely ornament over a faded two-lane road with more dirt, rocks, and weeds than asphalt. It had been several hours since the last stop. *We could use a diversion*, I thought. *Let's find this place, and we can get out and stretch our legs, take some pictures, and move on.*

I cautiously drove down the single-lane road filled with broken-down homes, tilting fences, and waist-high weeds, looking diligently for the sacred grave of Sacajawea. The sign we had found appeared to be a solo effort by the county or Indian reservation officials to get tourists to visit. No other sign, notecard, or clue was visible as we drove several miles deeper into the Indian reservation lands.

What we did see was beyond depressing. We observed family after family of Native Americans living out of beat-up trailers and huts or driving twenty-year-old trucks. Kids were playing in the dirt. We saw trash and abandoned property everywhere. Signs were rusty, buildings were empty, and windows were smashed. Roads were past disrepair, and there were no signs of modern conveniences in any direction. We drove on, looking left, right, and behind for any evidence of Sacajawea's grave site, but after fifteen minutes and four miles of wandering the countryside, we gave up. (Later, on another trip, I found it. I took pictures and video and texted my kids the details from the road. It wasn't marked at all; it was just out in a field, surrounded by an eight-foot marble statue, a historical plaque, and some flags.)

What our family found on that brief excursion was something much different from a tribute to one of the most remarkable women in our nation's history. We discovered the danger of living our lives only in the past or future tense, lost in the present.

> You must know where you came from yesterday, know
> where you are today, to know where you're going tomorrow.
>
> CREE SAYING

It's such a temptation to see only our past accomplishments or mistakes. We can live our current lives under the shadow of a long-ago moment of success or failure. It's also common for some of us to grow so exhausted that we give up on the present circumstances of our lives and retreat to a fantasy world of future hopes and dreams, ignoring today's realities.

I was reminded that we need to remain sober minded, as the Bible says—alert and aware of the challenges we face as families day-to-day. We can't be consumed with our past losses or gains. And we can't be dreamily hopeful that a winning lottery ticket or financial windfall will appear so that all our problems will magically disappear. Life needs to be lived, not survived. Today needs to be essential to us, not just another necessary detail to get through so we can make it to our next major life goal.

I realized that I could easily be drawn into a life that reflected the depression and despair surrounding us on this reservation—the despair of someone who has gotten a bad deal but feels trapped and unable to change things. But I didn't want that, and I didn't want my kids to learn that from me. So I made a personal resolution. I determined to remember this little side trip from the highway to the back road. By God's grace, I would move out of my past and into the present—not just on this vacation, but also back in Nashville in my regular struggles with work, ministry, and my overcrowded calendar.

Colorado Calls

Driving south out of Indian country into northern Colorado, we left the interstates for two-lane highways and the intimacy of smaller towns and less-traveled roads. Following Wyoming's Highway 130 to 230 south of I-80 to the state line, we cruised through the high plains and rugged mountains as we moved ever closer to my beloved Colorado Rockies. I took a great cutoff down Colorado State Highway 125 and did my best to keep my family from an epidemic of car sickness, navigating thirty miles of switchbacks and triple S curves at no more than thirty-five or forty miles per hour. The scenery was shifting from the drier elevated plains to the lush pine forests of the mountains, and the road was now hugging a wall sheared out of solid rock on one side, with a mountain stream and forested valley on the other.

We were in the remote northern edge of the Colorado Rockies, and I was getting excited. This was familiar country for me. I had driven these roads, skied on these mountains, and explored this area for more than three decades. It was great to be back—and fantastic to get to share this with my family. We were planning to spend the night at Granby, Colorado, before driving into Rocky Mountain National Park the next day. Granby was one of my favorites, as it was just far enough away from the après-ski scene at Winter Park to avoid the tourist buses and rush of flatlanders looking for trinkets and T-shirts to buy. Granby was also at the base of two great lakes and was the only southern entrance to Rocky Mountain National Park. It boasted mind-bending beauty from the snow-crested peaks that surrounded the valley as far as the eye could see.

We stopped at a fifties-era restored motel with a neon sign and twenty-five rooms. The price was sixty-five dollars for all five of us to crash in a "suite" that had a pullout sofa and a queen bed. Perfect! I was juiced. I knew in the morning we would be entering Rocky Mountain National Park and driving up the world-famous Trail Ridge Road across the very top of the Rockies. At over 12,000 feet, it represents not only a modern marvel of engineering but a hair-raising view, as vehicles drive literally twenty-four inches from the paved edge of a vast cliff face—something you get to do repeatedly as you navigate the road from either side.

I hardly slept that night. I couldn't tell if it was the large volume of Mongolian beef I had consumed at Granby's only Chinese restaurant (Caleb's choice) or if it was my excitement about the day ahead. Trail Ridge Road is arguably the most beautiful road in the world. Its panoramic mountain vistas allow you to see fifty to seventy-five miles on a clear day. The highest road in the United States, it represented another iconic moment for us to share as a family. Like Glacier or Yellowstone, Rocky Mountain National Park (RMNP) is an essential visit for anyone who wants to gain a sense of the vast wilderness beauty still out there waiting to be discovered. The thing that makes RMNP so special is its alpine tundra ecosystem. This supersensitive and breathtakingly beautiful tip of life on the very top of our highest mountain peaks is so rare and so fragile and yet so accessible at RMNP. Carefully protected paths and spaces have been preserved so generations of travelers, tourists, and explorers can see, smell, and feel the breath of heaven while still here on earth. I love it.

I had felt a nudge from God in the night. Or maybe it was just indigestion; I was so hyped that I couldn't tell for sure. The nudge suggested I should get up very early and get the family awake, fed, and in the SUV by dawn. After a long day on the road yesterday, I fought that nudge a bit. Maybe I was just projecting my own excitement to share RMNP with my kids so much that I was spiritualizing it. But as I rose quietly in the two-room suite, I felt it again. A nudge, as if God were prodding me to get up, get moving. He had something special for us today. I muttered something like, *Okay, but if this is a bust, I'm blaming you.*

Friday, July 2
Bethany's Moose or Dad's Indigestion

Obeying that nudge, I reluctantly woke everyone. As I did, I noticed the fog was so dense outside that I couldn't see the SUV parked ten feet in front of our door. It was thicker than any I had ever seen, like in a scene out of a pirate movie off the New England coast. Fog was not a welcome part of the beautiful drive, mountain vistas, and treasured family moments I had planned that morning, yet I felt the nudge again, telling me not to delay. This time the message was even stronger and clearer: *Tell them I have something special to show Bethany this morning, but all three will see something just for them today.*

Okay, here it was. God was nudging me, but if I responded to the specific instructions to share this message with my family, I ran the almost certain risk of them seeing me as the weird, "over-spiritual" dad. My wife would most likely roll her eyes at me, and my kids would be convinced that I was caught up in yet another of my manic, caffeine-induced exuberant outbursts, the kind that I had been known to exhibit occasionally when close to nature as beautiful as RMNP. I was afraid that I would botch this important opportunity with what my kids deemed another fanatical "Dad moment"—quite human and sincere, but judged by them to be sincerely wrong nonetheless.

I didn't want that. This was too important. Bethany had gotten better over the past nine months, but she was not well. She still struggled with trusting God to be interested in her. She often felt left out of his plans and wondered if he really heard prayers at all. She thought maybe God was just a powerful, all-present force that contained the universe and waited for us all to die before we could see, sense, or know him. We had discussed these issues but never resolved them.

I felt like God was prodding me to share with her and the rest of my family that, despite the cotton-thick fog outside, despite my emotional exuberance at being in the Rockies, this was a God and Bethany thing. A divine "date," if you will. A specific way for God to show Bethany, once and for all, that he was listening and that he was concerned about her—about her wants, her needs, and her desires.

Bethany had been wanting to see a moose in the wild now for over a week. The entire time we were in Canada, she had been relentless in her pursuit of capturing one on camera. Each hike, each morning by our creek-side cabin, or with every lake we explored, she was ready, looking, seeking, and hoping to find a moose, her favorite animal.

I had spent hundreds of hours in the woods and around the mountains and lakes of Canada and Colorado, but I had only seen a moose two or three times in more than thirty years. They were rare here, much less common than in Vermont or New Hampshire. I had cautioned Bethany not to get her hopes up too high, knowing that no matter how much she wanted to see one in the wild, it was going to be unlikely if not impossible on our short road trip. For one thing, moose are incredibly elusive in the wild, avoiding people, roads, and activity. For another, they are dangerous. You don't want to approach a moose on a trail or in the woods, as they can be deadly—much worse than bears or other, more obvious predators. Moose are huge, often over a thousand pounds and six to eight feet or more at the shoulder. Their antler racks are the size of car bumpers, and they have necks thicker than my waist. You just don't walk up to them and ask them to pose for a nice picture.

I knew that RMNP had a few moose, but it was more of an elk, deer, bear, bighorn sheep, and occasional eagle kind of place. Moose really like wetlands, not jagged mountain peaks and alpine tundra. I remembered that RMNP had a beautiful ten-mile river valley on its western edge, and it was possible some moose might like to graze on its banks. But that would happen infrequently, especially now, in the midst of July's peak summer tourist season. Lots of cars, RVs, and people, all very noisy, did not create a great environment to discover one of nature's most elusive and dangerous mammals. So with that in mind, I was extremely hesitant to suggest to Bethany that God would arrange for her to see and photograph a moose today. I mean, that's crazy talk—the kind of stuff that could wound her more and convince her that my faith and my God were as silly as the TV evangelists she made fun of with her friends.

I sighed deeply.

The nudge from God would not go away, so I told her most of what God told me to. Something like this: "Bethany, I know this sounds crazy, but I think God woke me up early to get us all on the road so that he could show you something really special along the way. Something you have been asking him for this entire vacation but have not seen. Something that you have specifically prayed to him about. If we go right now, I think your prayer will be answered today."

There, I said it. At least most of it. No, I didn't actually say she would see a moose today, but I sure hinted enough to make it clear to our entire family that's what I was talking about. The reality was, by the end of the day, I would either be seen as a legit "heard from God" kind of dad, or a total religious windbag. I had stepped out of my comfort zone for sure on this one. As predicted, my wife rolled her eyes, as if to say, "What do you think you're doing saying stuff like that?"

I didn't really know. I just felt the nudge and knew I had to follow it.

Of Fog and Faith

We repacked our dozens of bags, suitcases, trinkets, and snacks and piled in the SUV. We grabbed some jackets, hats, and cameras and drove off into the murky fog. It was 6 a.m., local time.

The fog was intense, and the twenty miles up from Granby to the west entrance of Rocky Mountain National Park were a bit underwhelming. Fog blocked the views of the pristine lakes to our right, as well as the snowcapped peaks of the 12,000-foot Arapaho National Forest mountains that bumped up to RMNP. It blocked the cute lake villages and old cabins; it blocked the views of the valley and the retro-cool tourist town of Grand Lake. It blocked the view of the forest and the trees, and it blocked my view of the road beyond the fifteen feet of pavement my headlights could illuminate. It was cold, wet, and damp. Forty degrees, with misty clouds of almost frozen condensation on our windshield. And I was looking for a moose.

We crossed the visitor's entrance, and the fog was relentless— maybe even thicker than when we'd started out in Granby forty-five minutes before. I was starting to get really concerned. I was worried that all that talk and spirituality had just been indigestion and that I was about to crash and burn in an epic way. Meanwhile, Paige was quietly riding beside me in the front passenger seat. I knew she was cautiously optimistic, but she wasn't talking about it. Though she wasn't given to hearing these kinds of messages from God, she knew from experience that God sometimes spoke to me this way, and she was willing to let me follow my spiritual hunch.

I drove the first ten miles as slowly as humanly possible. I admit I was stalling. If the sun got high enough and strong enough, it would burn through the fog, and then we would be able to see the valley to our right. The valley where there might be a moose. I could tell that Bethany was anxious, hopeful for the first time in a while that maybe she would have a chance at capturing a moose on her camera—and, more important, hopeful for a touch from God reminding her that she was special, that he did care, that her needs and wants were vital to him. That she wasn't alone, that God would provide, that he would meet all her desires, and that her dad wasn't entirely insane . . .

After eight miles and thirty minutes of creeping through the valley, after pausing at three road turnoffs to peer into the fog-shrouded valley, I was done. No moose today. I was wrong.

I didn't say anything out loud, but I was thinking it: *Dude, you're crazy. You want so desperately for your daughter to see a moose and embrace your faith and heal from something awful that you cooked up this entire road-trip idea on your own dime. You convinced yourself and your family that God would position a moose on a specific day at a specific time just to show Bethany that he cares, that he exists. Now if she doesn't see one, she'll be crushed. This could be a disaster.*

Despite my doubts, I drove on. The fog persisted, but I knew that as we went into the elevated areas of the park, the drier air would dissipate the fog, giving us a better view for the rest of the drive. I also knew no moose would be that high in the park. Our only chance had been in the valley below. I resigned myself to being at least partially nuts and went on, smiling and chatting up Bethany and the kids as if nothing were amiss.

Until I felt the nudge once more. *Again?* I thought.

I could almost hear the words in my head: *Pull over, now!* They were commanding, insistent, and firm, so I did it. I obeyed the voice and drove off to the left shoulder of the road. I was stopped a few feet off the asphalt and looking right into the oncoming lane of traffic, stuck now next to a thick stand of trees. I rolled down my window and listened intently to hear something, anything. Not a sound.

I got out; the fog was as thick as ever. "Bethany," I whispered, "get your camera. I've got a feeling." We all jumped out and quietly walked to our left, toward a stand of trees and a bluff overlooking the valley below. We couldn't see much of anything, due to the summer tree coverage and the dense, unrelenting fog. But because I had been around this general area before, I believed we were close to the edge of the tree line. As we approached, I saw the fog pull back like a curtain. There, about twenty-five feet from us, was a huge female moose drinking and grazing by the edge of the valley—directly across from Bethany.

I almost threw up.

It was amazing. It was miraculous. It was God. I felt the impossible touch of the divine as it reached into my daughter's heart and grabbed her! God was shouting at her, *I love you, I love you, I love you, Bethany Rose! I want to be near you! I want to touch your hurts and heal all your pain!* It couldn't be ignored; it couldn't be fabricated, faked, or arranged. It had to be God!

I felt weak in the knees, weary and worn from the burden of it all. I realized I had been trying so hard to be the perfect dad, husband, and pastor. I had hoped and dreamed and tried to be all that I could be to Bethany so she would believe, so she would trust in God by my example. But in the end, I wasn't enough. It took God showing up to win her heart.

Bethany was taking pictures as fast as her fingers could press the button. She was enthralled, as if a small child had taken over her body and mind and heart. She was smiling, laughing, and full of genuine and unrestrained joy. I hadn't seen that in her face for a year or more. She was happy, and all traces of cynicism and sarcasm were gone from her face. She was free, released from whatever lies the darkness in her mind had told her about the nature of God.

I could tell the lie was exposed, broken. The truth of God was setting her free. God did care; God was involved; God would meet and exceed her every expectation. This moose in the valley was so perfect, so specific, so exactly what she had prayed for, that it couldn't be ignored, brushed away, or contrived as coincidence. It was God. Issue settled. Life changed. Hope renewed.

Bethany had her moose . . . and I wasn't crazy.

Moose Messages

This experience taught me like no other to listen carefully for God's nudges. His Holy Spirit will direct us, despite ourselves. The more we sense his presence and leading, the better we can drive our families' SUVs along the best and most beautiful road of life. The path God has prescribed for each of us is so unique and so intentional that if we're not careful, we can miss it, out of fatigue, frustration, or fear. We must be sensitive to the leading of God. That means quieting ourselves enough to listen, to hear, and to confirm that God is talking—not the take-out food.

I almost bailed on the moose idea, but by God's grace I didn't. We all can get in the way of what God wants to do in our kids' lives, but the closer we stay to his Word and his presence, the better we can become at hearing his voice and following his nudges for ourselves and our families.

This is not an exact science or an exercise of personal powerful faith; it is instead a willingness to follow where God leads. Let him handle the details. Let him arrange for the miracles. Our job is just to trust and obey. Our kids will get the message.

I don't know what your "Bethany" is like or how challenging your home or family life has become. We each have our own struggles. But I think the same truth from my experience can apply to yours, too. I knew that I couldn't fix Bethany or heal her pain. No matter how much I prayed, how much I strived to be the best dad in the world, it wouldn't bring back her innocence or hope or joy. God alone could do that.

He only asked me to be a spokesman for him, which is something he asks of us all. I am so glad I surrendered my pride long enough for God to do what he had planned in my daughter's life that foggy morning outside Granby, Colorado. So grateful that God kept nudging me until I acted. If that's faith, then that means anyone can be faithful to God. If I can, you can.

The key is spending time in his Word—reading the Bible and listening to what you sense him telling you. Ask God to show you what you need to know for this day, for your life, for your family, for the future. Keep a journal or notepad handy, and be prepared to write some stuff down. Be ready to hear from God.

He is always speaking to us. It's just so loud in our heads that we rarely hear him. Yet if we can't hear him for ourselves, we will never be able to teach our kids or lead our families with anything but our own wisdom and strength . . . and that is beyond exhausting.

It's impossible.

[Jesus] said, "What is impossible with man is possible with God." LUKE 18:27, ESV

BETHANY'S STORY

Ask, and it will be given to you; seek, and you will find; knock, and it will be opened to you.   MATTHEW 7:7, ESV

My dad has always come home from road trips in a joyous awe of the many things he has seen—breathtaking mountain ranges reaching up to heaven, snow piled several feet high, the mellow rush of forest creeks, and of course, exotic wildlife. Ever since I can remember, I have been intrigued by the diversity of the earth's creatures. When I was eight, I remember keeping a journal filled with photos and fun facts of animals around the world. Naturally, when Dad arrived home with more stories than luggage, I was eager to push past the mountain descriptions and hear about the newest roadside critters.

When I found out our family was going to be driving up to Banff National Park in Canada, I was out of my mind. I was going on my first major road trip, but more than that, I was going to stumble into a new land of adventure and sights I had only heard about. I was going to experience the apparent "amazingness" my dad had dangled in front of me like my favorite pie. It was my time to really understand—to taste how wonderful this pie really was.

The day we left I was ready with my camera. Although I knew we wouldn't reach the Canadian border for several days, my excitement had me looking forward to even the most miniscule of events, like pulling over at Indian reservation gas stations in central Montana. I didn't care how small; I wanted the full experience.

Once we actually crossed the Canadian border, my camera was dead from the couple hundred roadside photos of nothing I had continued to snap as a means of occupying myself through the hours of driving. Realizing I had wasted the battery, I was mad that I might miss capturing something great. But to my surprise and disappointment, the remainder of our travel into Banff National Park left me with no reason to wish my camera back to life. Where was all the wildlife? The elk running through meadows, bears with claws out to defend their cubs, and cute Canadian chipmunks? Most important to me, where were the moose? As odd as the presence of a moose in the "must see" category may seem, I was determined to have a firsthand look at one—and a picture to prove it. Unfortunately, moose are a rare sight to behold in the wild, and knowing that, my dad attempted to keep my expectations at bay. However, being the stubborn person I have always been, I was bound and determined. I honestly believed I would see one.

We arrived at our cabin by Lake Louise, hidden in a community of several identical cottages settled within a forest of trees and enclosed by abandoned train tracks and rushing mountain water. It was beautiful, and the views only escalated as our visit went along.

Each morning my dad woke us up at six to go exploring. We would sleepily get out of bed, pull on layers of clothes to shield our bodies from the frigid snowy air, strap on our hiking boots and backpacks, and drive out to the starting line of our winding eight-mile trails. Each path Dad led us on was unique in its landscape. What would begin as a concrete sidewalk would quickly morph to resemble a grassy African plain, which within half a mile shifted back into a snowy forest. Then, after climbing up a steep hill, we would be standing on a desert of rock and mineral sediment, only to look up and realize we were at eye level with each cloud and passing plane. Everywhere we went I anticipated something new to feast my eyes on, all the while double-checking for any brown antlers poking through the evergreen branches.

By the end of our week roaming the vast Canadian terrain, riding across glaciers, making silly faces for the camera in front of hundred-foot-high waterfalls, and squealing in delight at wandering elk, I was amazed but still not completely satisfied. My heart was lost to the majesty of God's incredible handiwork, and I was not ready to say good-bye. Not only that, but I had yet to cross paths with a moose.

Even in writing this out, my strong desire to see a moose comes across as odd—almost humorous. I mean, honestly, what was the big deal? Well, in the grand scheme of life, seeing a moose was not a big deal. The big deal was God. I wanted to feel him in a new way. God had always been more of a legendary character to me. I had grown up in church singing songs about him and had listened to countless pastors talk about how great he is, but the more I thought about God on my own, the clearer it became to me that he was only that—someone I heard other people talking about. Although I should have been thankful for the opportunity to learn about Jesus when people on the other side of the world are locked up for holding a Bible, I wasn't.

I am a person who needs to see something to believe it. I couldn't fully believe in a God I had never seen to be real for myself. I needed God to speak to *me*, not to a room full of dressed-up churchgoers. At school, I always felt like another face in the crowd, if not completely invisible, and I couldn't put my faith in someone who looked at me as another passing figure. Dad always talked about the close presence of God he always felt in nature—the kind that is just short of tangible. He had promised each of us our special moment, but as far as I could see, that promise was waiting, lifeless, a couple of steps ahead of me.

As we drove into Rocky Mountain National Park, I could see the final stretch of pines scattered along the road. My dad was half-jokingly telling us to wave our good-byes out the window to the wild terrain, because within minutes, it would be out of our sight for the remainder of the trip. As our family's Honda Pilot carried us along the street, I sat silent. This trip had been incredible. Unforgettable. All the clichés people use about a wonderful time really described how I felt, but there was a portion of my heart that felt wilted—like a flower abandoned while it tried to bloom. I wasn't angry; there was no cursing in my thoughts. It was how I would feel if I had bought a lottery ticket and was holding my breath as the winning number was drawn. Digit by digit and breath by breath, I waited. Of course I would feel a pang of disappointment if the number on my ticket didn't match the winning combination, but I would know I had neither gained nor lost anything.

All those emotions were running through me as my dad slammed on his brakes and pulled over. *What in the world?* I thought as I pulled my earbuds out and turned to see what was happening. My mom, sister, and brother all looked up in mutual confusion, but my dad offered no explanation. Instead he told us to get our cameras out and follow him. My dad is often spontaneous like this, so my family has learned to listen first and ask questions later.

We scrambled to find our cameras and throw our shoes back on before we lost sight of our dad, who was already halfway down the nonexistent trail. "Shhh . . . be very quiet and turn your flash off," he commanded as we caught up with him. I didn't know what we were being quiet about or what I was supposed to be taking a picture of, but I did as I was told—which, when looking at my rebellious and defiant history, was a rarity itself. Yet somehow I knew that whatever my dad had led us to, it was important. Something I would regret missing.

We found ourselves gathered in a small opening of a road-side forest. But instead of the trees thickening into a mass of prickly branches and tall wooden trunks, the land opened up to a vast green valley overtaken by twisting weeds and shoulder-high grass still glittering with morning dew. It was beautiful and peaceful. The kind of place you would find a young girl lying under the sun in a bright sundress, blowing her wishes free on a dandelion, feeling nothing but joy. As I stood taking in the view, I let my eyes follow the direction of my dad's finger pointing to a spot about ten yards in front of us. It was a moose. She was positioned in plain sight, not bothered by the crowd that was beginning to form around her. Seven feet tall, fully tan, broad in the shoulders, with antlers that could easily take down the strongest of predators, she stood quietly chewing on her morning leaves.

I took easily fifty photos of her while we watched. I couldn't get over the fact that I was seeing this moose. My grandparents, who had been to the mountains on a dozen occasions, had never seen a moose. People kept telling me to give it up, and yet here I was as a fifteen-year-old watching my childhood *Animal Planet* videos come to life. I knew it was probably a once-in-a-lifetime moment, and I wanted to savor it. We stood as silent statues for the next ten minutes or so, afraid that any snap of a fallen tree branch would expose our presence and send the moose away, startled. But she never moved more than a few feet.

If we hadn't been thousands of miles away from home, we probably would have sat back and watched until sundown. Eventually, though, we reluctantly took a last look at our miraculous discovery and piled back into the car. I buckled my seat belt, situated myself between pillows and blankets, and hit play on my iPod. *Wow*, I thought, smiling to myself, as I closed my eyes to sleep.

Not too long after we were on the road again, my dad began talking about the moose. "That really was something. That moose was just for you, Bethany. What do you think about that?"

"Well, it was awesome! I mean, you said I wouldn't see a moose, but I did. We all did."

Quickly realizing that I wasn't grasping the representative reality behind the moose, he began telling me how he couldn't see that moose from the road. He had been praying on our way out that morning, and he felt God nudge him to pull over. He thought he might be crazy, but he couldn't shake the thought, so he pulled over. Sure enough, God wasn't just playing mind games with my dad. "That moose was for you, Bethany," he said again.

Up until that point I hadn't even thought about what my dad was saying, but it all made sense. Even though at the time I was still on the teeter-totter of faith in a personal relationship with God, in that moment it clicked not only in my mind but in my spirit. My dad was right—that moose was for me. God had heard my prayers all along. He knew I needed a visual sign to feel close to him, and he gave it to me. The sad part is that I almost missed it. No, actually, I did miss it, and all because I had an idea of what God needed to do to show up for me. The irony is that I didn't have an exact scenario in mind, but it definitely wasn't pulling over on the side of a strange road, walking into a forest, and stumbling upon a gentle moose.

I think that happens to us a lot. We keep asking for God to show up, to answer our prayers, and we only end up frustrated or cursing at the wind when our heart cries go unheard. But God does answer. He hears all our prayers, and we only miss his responses because we are expecting him to show up according to our predetermined plans. We have to realize that God is not going by our plans. He already has plans—the perfect plans—and if we aren't careful, we will miss them like I did with the moose.

Ultimately, God is alive and active, and he's well aware of our needs. He will always answer—not because we are entitled, but because he loves us. Internally, I had let myself become high and mighty to the point that I believed God owed it to me to respond. God owes us nothing, because he already gave us everything. That is one of the amazing things I have since learned about God. He wants to give us everything.

When we feel like our prayers have been deemed unimportant in God's eyes, we have to learn to quiet ourselves and remember what he has told us. Then we wait patiently in prayer, keeping our spiritual eyes open to the unexpected yet wonderful ways God will show up.

I know the plans I have for you, declares the Lord, plans for welfare and not for evil, to give you a future and a hope.

JEREMIAH 29:11, ESV

TWELVE

CALEB'S CLIMB AND JESSICA'S RAINBOW

Thou hast made us for thyself, O Lord, and our hearts are restless till they find rest in thee.

ST. AUGUSTINE OF HIPPO, *THE CONFESSIONS OF ST. AUGUSTINE*

BETHANY WAS ALL ear-to-ear smiles and white teeth, laughing and joyful as we turned to head back to our SUV and start up the mountain to the top and into Estes Park. She was excitedly sharing her pictures in the camera's viewfinder as we walked back to the road. "Dad! Look at this one. See how close I got for this one! It was a girl moose, Dad, my favorite!!" She was giddy with excitement, with adrenaline—with hope. After ten days and five thousand miles, she had found her moose, and it had been worth the wait. Now that was a metaphor worth remembering for a teenage daughter.

God knew what he was up to, and I was just now able to step back far enough from the action to see the beauty of his divine and strategic plan. This faith stuff was beginning to feel like the verses I knew from the Bible:

> Take my yoke upon you, and learn from me, for I am gentle and lowly in heart, and you will find rest for your souls. For my yoke is easy, and my burden is light.
>
> MATTHEW 11:29-30 (ESV)

It seemed that God was quite capable of connecting the "faith dots" in my daughter. I just needed to remain faithful to pray, and faithful to listen and obey. The rest, it appeared, was already covered. God had a plan. I didn't need to expend all my energy in making it happen. When Jesus said his burden was light, he meant that we don't carry the responsibility for salvation. I could relax in the understanding that God was in control, not just of my life but of my kids' lives. Grace would have to be enough for them, just as it had to be for me. I felt my chest begin to let go of a deep breath that I guess I had been holding since last October. Bethany was going to be okay.

Who knew what else would be discovered on this magical day? I had no idea, but I was sure of one thing—I didn't want to miss it. I watched in the rearview mirror as Bethany scrolled through her camera shots. I saw what looked like a shadow come off her face and out of her eyes, and I saw the beauty of peace flood into her. It was awesome. God showed up, and I got to watch him do another miracle. This time, it was my little girl he healed.

High-Altitude Hiking

We ducked back out onto the highway. The traffic was getting heavy and the sky was lightening as we drove up the slow, steady switch-backs of Trail Ridge Road. Gradually we emerged above the fog, and the blue-on-blue sky took our breath away. It's not easy to describe the view of an entire range of mountain peaks poking up over the fluffy fog and clouds gathered in the valleys below, but I'll try.

Picture snowcapped stone spires with miniature green bumps and fuzz (the massive forests on their edges), dotted with outcrop-pings of rock and sheer stone walls, rising up out of a soupy cotton horizon. Imagine the searingly bright golden sunlight without any filters—no clouds, no smog, no smoke, no buildings between you and it, no restrictions to its glare, and no reduction in its power. The sun is blazing across the sky and feels like it's closer to you than ever before . . . because it is.

The air gets clearer the higher you drive; the sky is bluer and the sun brighter. The earth starts to bend a little on the edges of your view of the horizon, and you realize you're going so high that you can begin to sense that the earth is indeed a sphere. The wind starts to really blow, gently at first, then with more insistence as you go higher. The trees are greener, the water is fresher, the birds are all louder, and the senses that you have used your whole life start to wake up.

Hearing, smell, vision, touch—everything starts to rev up. You sense that until now, you have only been about half alive. Today, right now, you're sensing that you could become fully alive, and it's like sugar, caffeine, and pure energy all combined into something indescribably perfect. You start to wonder if you could fly, or at least climb up that beautiful mountain there on the right. You pull over at the next scenic overlook and dash out of the car to snap some pictures and suck in all this natural goodness deep down into the very core of your soul. You want to capture it forever!

Then you bend over and cough, gagging and almost retching as you realize you have no air to breathe and your head feels like it was hit by a hammer. You're seeing blue spots, and your legs feel as if they might be made of rubber. Wobbly, you try to reorient your vision, but you can't. The world is swimming, bouncing, and jumping around as you try to sit or find your way back to the car. *Woozy* is a good word for it.

No, you're not dying. It's just that you have decided, like me, to stop at 10,000 feet, jump out of your car, and run to the edge of a short trail to see the sights and snap some pictures. But your lungs couldn't keep up with your now-fuzzy brain, due to a lack of oxygen in your blood. Your body is no longer impressed with the view but rather interested in sitting down until it can get enough oxygen to keep you alive long enough to enjoy that beautiful view.

As you struggle to catch your breath, it dawns on you that your kids are running around without a care in the world. They are excited about all the cool things they can see, snapping pictures and feeding the little chipmunk-like creatures all around the stone balcony on the overlook. They are oblivious to the fact that you are nearly in a coma, sipping air like your lungs have been reduced to the size of a quarter. Slowly, after about ninety seconds, the world realigns and you can actually form words and breathe naturally again.

Yes, high-altitude hiking is not for the uninitiated or the lung-compromised among us, so be warned. If you're a flatlander (someone who lives 1,500 feet or less above sea level), the exploration of mountains and elevated views should be embraced gingerly. It usually takes two to three days for flatlanders to acclimate to the reduced oxygen levels and altitude before they are comfortably able to take simple hikes without feeling like they have a hangover.

Some people never really adjust and need to take it easy, but most folks under fifty years of age have no problem. Kids rarely notice anything. However, if you go to the top of Trail Ridge Road, both adults and kids are going to notice the effect on their bodies. At over 11,000 feet, it's seriously high and will take some getting used to. Don't just jump out and start hiking.

Caleb's Climb

We stopped and had a blast at the Alpine Visitor's Center and gift shop at the top of Trail Ridge Road. The day we visited was sunny, windy, and cool—about forty-five degrees with a stiff, thirty-mile-per-hour breeze out of the west. We stopped at the visitor's center, had some hot chocolate and coffee, and took potty breaks. Caleb was starting to get excited. We were in the tundra now, so far up that trees were unable to live at this height due to wind and lack of oxygen. The ancient gray rocks around us were smooth from exposure to the constant wind, rain, and snow.

We were driving slowly across the winding, narrow highway when we saw a pull-off for a scenic overlook. Dropping off a cliff about 3,000 feet to our right was a valley with some lakes and rivers draining from the mountains nearby. The kids wanted pictures, and so did I. When we jumped out, Caleb saw a trail across the road that went up a winding slope to the very top of the mountainside. He wanted to take it.

Warily, I sucked in a deep breath. I knew we were now pushing 12,000 feet, and the trail went up? I could definitely feel the altitude, but with the thirty pounds I had lost that spring and my walking regimen, I was doing better than I had feared. I decided to give it a go. I shouted at Caleb (you have to shout at such a height due to the wind) that I would follow if he wanted to try the trail. I grabbed my wool cap and gloves, wrapped my North Face jacket over my sweat-shirt, and felt I was as ready as I would ever be. Caleb was thirteen and full of "vim and vinegar," as my grandpa used to say. He wasn't even taking a deep breath yet.

The wind was behind us as we climbed up the rock-strewn trail. There were a surprising number of people on the trail, all with various outfits—some very "together" and color coordinated, others a hodgepodge of old and new clothes, hastily layered to try to protect them against the unexpectedly cold July day. If they had come from Estes Park, the air temperature there could have been as high as 85°F already. Up here it was barely above freezing—37°F with a wind-chill factor of 15–20°F. That's seriously cold for summer.

Caleb didn't care. He was pushing on ahead of me, map in one hand and camera in the other. He had on his sunglasses, a hat, and his ever-present zip-up hoodie. I had layered as much as I could, but he seemed warmer in just his one layer than I was in several. Teenagers—they make me sick.

I pushed on, slowing down now as the air continued to thin. The wind seemed to be blowing harder, if that was possible. I was concerned that some of the smaller, lighter people might have trouble walking in this kind of wind. I'm guessing the gusts at times were in the 55–60 mph range. After about ten minutes, I almost couldn't feel my fingers or toes. But after twenty minutes, I was starting to enjoy the view a bit. We had emerged above it all, literally. The path had become a narrow strip of stones between the green and fragile tundra grasses dotted with flowers.

I could see a herd of elk about five hundred feet below us, lazily munching on grass and sunning themselves on the mountainside. They were up here for the day after spending the evening somewhere in the valley below. I knew they were massive creatures, five hundred pounds on average, with huge antlers and generally calm dispositions. The cars looked like toys below us, slowly following the gray ribbon of pavement.

Caleb was already at the very top of the half-mile trail, sitting on a rock outcropping that had a copper or brass inscription. A compass was marked in the stone, along with some hundred-year-old history lessons about the first explorers and settlers in the region. It was cool to be here with my son, and at last I could breathe again!

He was busy taking pictures and climbing the car-size boulders that made up the end of the trail. We were at the very tip-top of the mountain we had been driving around. You could see at least sixty miles in every direction, and the eastern grass plains of Colorado were stretching out to the north and east of our perch. Caleb was enthralled. His eyes were alight with the scene, and his heart was beating with more than blood. He was proud that he had been the first to scale these heights. Not his older sisters, not his mom, not his dad, but him. He had run ahead of us all; he had climbed it and conquered it. He alone—and that confidence fueled in him much more than a momentary warmth or sense of purpose. It was the beginning of developing a man's heart to explore and tame the world.

I saw all that and more in a flash. In the flicker of an eyelid and a quick intake of breath, I had an awareness that something really important was transmitted to my son in this spot. An almost imperceptible transfer of maturity had occurred. Like a personal mile marker, this mountain would be a stepping-stone for Caleb on his journey from boy to man.

I smiled, I laughed, and I even cried a little. God was doing some cool stuff today, that was for sure. Caleb couldn't see my eyes or my tears, since the wind was blowing a gale and my glasses were firmly fixed to my face. This was my private celebration. Just me and God, watching as my son stepped out of boyhood a bit more and discovered that he could climb a mountain.

We sat there, enjoying a view that few had found. The crowds of tourists were far below; the few hearty walkers had all turned back. We were alone, absorbing the lofty perspective usually reserved for eagles and jets. I had little to add to the delight of that moment. Like with Bethany's moose, this was God stuff, and words were just not necessary.

I didn't share with my son some great life lesson, explain to him how much I could tell this had impacted his self-confidence, tell him how living with God is like having this mountaintop perspective, or remind him how Jesus had often withdrawn to the mountains to pray. No, instead I just sat there, soaking it all up—the beauty, the view, the wind, and the air, clear and crisp as any on earth. I thanked God for the chance to be here with my son at this moment. It was more than I deserved and more than I could have hoped for.

We slowly pulled ourselves down from the rocks and returned to the stone trail. We walked carefully back down the path to our car on the side of the road. As we descended, the winds slowed, the oxygen level in the air rose, and the temperature warmed. It felt dull to be out of the elements, safe and sound back in our climate-controlled Honda. I was already missing the flush of red on my cheeks from the wind, the dripping of my nose from the cold, and the emotional rush of climbing something so high that nothing was above it anymore.

But we had to go home.

Caleb gushed to his mom and sisters about the phenomenal views, the cold wind, and the rugged rocks we had climbed. He showed them the pictures, and then he was back to his iPod. I wasn't upset; I wasn't even frustrated. I had just shared with my son one of the most amazing life experiences I could ever ask for. He was stoked, and his way of celebrating was to find the best possible music to match the world he had just encountered. I decided to let him simply rest and enjoy the view as we drove down into the mountain town and legendary trinket mecca that is Estes Park, Colorado.

As we drove on, we enjoyed the beauty of Rocky Mountain National Park's eastern slopes. Taking this path is like descending into a scene from one of the old TV Westerns like *Bonanza*. I couldn't help but hum the theme song as I drove. Now that we'd crossed the Continental Divide, the landscape was totally different. Water and grass gave way to rocks and red dirt. It was every bit as beautiful as the other side of the mountain, just radically different. If this side of the park was dubbed "cowboy," then the other side could be called "mountain man." The pine trees in particular were massive, and the aroma of pinecones and sap filled the air. Huge white-tailed deer roamed freely, and we noticed signs for bighorn sheep and bear. Tourists, buses, and RVs clogged the road as we slowly descended Trail Ridge.

It was good to be up at the top of the road early, and it was good to get out of there as soon as possible too. The crowds were growing on this fine Friday in July. At the request of my wife and daughters, we stopped for a brief shopping excursion. After that, we drove through and out of Estes Park, and then we motored south toward Denver and our next destination: Santa Fe.

We wanted to be back in Nashville by Sunday, so we had two days left to visit Santa Fe and get home. After our early-morning moose adventure, the long drive, and that high-altitude hike through the Rockies, the steady hum of the road and the vacant, uninterrupted prairie views were less than stimulating. By the time we hit the outskirts of Denver, I was the only one with my eyes still open.

We passed Denver by early afternoon on I-25 and set our sights on

New Mexico. I had chosen to go through Santa Fe on the way back so I could show my family the mission at El Santuario de Chimayo. It was a meaningful site for me that had changed my life on each of my previous three visits, and I was anxious to show my family the place where God had started to rearrange my understanding of him.

CALEB'S STORY

Canada was an unforgettable experience, and I had the pleasure to share it with my family. Some of the best parts on the trip included Bow Lake, which was my personal favorite lake. Along the side of it you could take a trail that stretched for what seemed like miles. It took you through multiple types of terrain, including a forested area along the bank of the lake, a desert with mounds of rocks scattered throughout to help you stay on the trail, mountainous areas with cliffs to overlook, and finally the grand finale led you to a waterfall with inuksuks everywhere, made by other people who had taken the very same trail. It was a very incredible experience to share with my family, especially with my cousins, since I usually see them only once a year.

Another highlight was to climb to the top of a mountain at Rocky Mountain National Park. I never knew how windy it could be at that altitude—or how treacherous storms could get, until I saw one brewing on the horizon. Once I finally reached the top (which took so much breath out of me), I was in awe of the view from above. I had to cling to the giant rock I stood on because the gusting winds kept trying to push me off. As my dad always says, "This is where God lives" (referring to Canada and the Rocky Mountains). At that moment I understood what he meant by that, since you can feel so much power being on a mountaintop. The trip was for sure something I could never forget and will probably remain one of the most epic road trips I will ever go on in my life.

Evening Rainbows and Broken Promises

By the time we hit Trinidad, Colorado, the sun was almost setting. Ahead of us, just over the border into New Mexico, we could see a massive July thunderstorm pounding the dry and dusty plains. Lightning was arcing across the sky, and the blackest of black clouds loomed low over the horizon. Caleb and Bethany got a bit nervous, and even Jessica looked worried. After all the severe weather we had driven through on the way out a week and half earlier, we had developed a healthy respect, even fear, of thunderstorms.

Jessica leaned forward and seemed to really wake up, while the others were concerned but too tired to care much. We had been driving on the interstate now for hundreds of miles; the road was putting everyone into a very mellow mood. But Jessica seemed wide-awake. She was talking about the Spanish classes she'd taken in her junior high and freshman years of school. She was excited to be able to visit such an ancient and historical town, and she wanted to know more about the culture, the art, the history, the food, and the atmosphere of a Southwestern city that was older than our nation. I tried to tell her, but it was impossible to summarize the nuances of a city as beautiful and unique as Santa Fe.

Along the way we descended the last great mountain pass (Raton Pass), leaving Colorado and entering New Mexico. As the sun set, we ran straight into a nasty storm. Thunderstorms on the prairie are much more violent than in the hills and hollers of Tennessee. The rain lashed across the road, and wind bent the few trees almost in half. This was a serious storm cell and, like the others we had driven through, could produce tornadoes.

In the strobe-like flashes of lightning, Jessica and I scanned the dark skies for any sign of a funnel cloud. She was careful to keep a wary eye out as I drove. The others were pretty much asleep, and I felt like she was my copilot. As we traveled along this long, flat stretch of interstate in northern New Mexico, suddenly Jessica noticed something off to the east—an incredibly bright, huge, complete rainbow, with a clear beginning and a clear end. It was like a neon sign, so bright in contrast to the black clouds behind it. It was the most beautiful rainbow I have ever witnessed. Within a few minutes, Jessica had taken several pictures and had spotted a second rainbow behind it. In five more miles, a third rainbow appeared. Then the sun dipped below the horizon, and all the color drained from the sky.

As we drove on, I realized how rare that sight had to be. I had never seen three rainbows at one time. Beyond that, their color and vibrancy were extraordinary, popping out against the black sky. They shone with a superbright, surreal illumination for the last three or four minutes of daylight. It was like a beautiful fireworks display just for us.

The fact that my oldest daughter had roused herself from her pillowed nest, at the tail end of a day when we'd spent fourteen hours on the road, told me she was more than a little intrigued by the intense bursts of color outside our SUV. She was suddenly very alert to what was happening around us, no longer reserved or drowsy. It had to be due to the unusual appearance of the rainbows.

I thought about the incredible moments we had shared already today and the excitement the rainbows had brought to Jessica. *God*, I asked, *was that for her?* His answer was a whisper, like my nudges earlier that day: *Yes*.

Jessica is the oldest child, the worrier, even a bit of a control freak. She needed to know that the storms were not going to hurt her or her family. I think God was telling her that the passage ahead was safe. The next season of her life might look stormy and might be a bit uncomfortable, but she was exactly where she was supposed to be. God's promise was being upheld, and he was reassuring Jessica of his ability to keep a promise—an idea she had struggled to trust over the years.

Jessica was often cynical, opting to be sarcastic instead of optimistic about the future. This attitude sprang from what she perceived as broken promises from me, Paige, or her friends and family. Being a literalist, Jessica would often take the smallest of promises to extremes. When she was a little girl, if we gave even a hint of a promise to get ice cream on a shopping day and then weren't able to follow through, she would express long, deep resentment. As she got older, she was careful to catalog the promises we made about trips or special vacations, and if financial circumstances happened to interrupt those plans, she would be angry for weeks. Those normal moments of disappointment were compounded by my sunny personality, which could often create promises out of what were just possibilities. Jessica, it seemed, kept a mental checklist of those broken promises (both perceived and actual) that both Paige and I had made.

Jessica was expecting people to fail her, looking to find fault in anyone who made promises they couldn't or wouldn't keep. Having little patience for these betrayals, she chose not to depend on others. She had decided that she could count on herself and no one else.

God saw her pain. He noticed her suffering. And he used a miraculous, triple rainbow to show Jessica that he is the one who always, always keeps his promises. It was as if God knew my daughter needed this reminder that it's okay to trust, to hope, to believe. Not all promises are broken. This very trip was a promise kept by her parents. But no matter how often others may disappoint us, God himself remains trustworthy. His promises are never broken.

This was God's message to Jessica, and the exclamation point on it all was the rare display of the triple rainbow. This unmistakable symbol of God's integrity was being delivered to a wonderfully straightforward young lady in exactly the right way for her to understand. God was teaching Jessica that she could rely on him for his promises to her, no matter what her earthly father or mother or friends had done. It was an illuminating truth for me— and a vital one for Jessica.

It made me as her father very aware of the powerful, painful disappointments I had caused in Jessica's life when I had walked away from her and her mother so many years before. Going forward, I needed to be extra-cautious about making promises that I couldn't keep or statements that I couldn't back up. Her faith in her heavenly Father was affected by the actions of her earthly one, and I had to make sure my words would be like those brilliant rainbows: light for my oldest child to see and believe and trust.

It was a simple but profound truth, which continues to shape the way I think about my oldest daughter. I am much more careful to keep every promise I make, or to slow down when I am about to promise anything to her, because I know that her faith and her understanding of God are shaped by my actions. Those rainbows helped me to grasp the deeper issues of Jessica's life and faith.

JESSICA'S STORY

Going to Canada the summer after my sophomore year of high school was a monumental experience. My priorities were and still are to see the world. This "epic road trip" was all I could think of before June. I remember I even got a new journal just to document all our travels. I did not want one moment of that time to be forgotten or spent in vain. I imprinted all the views in my mind. I would look at the valleys and clouds and say to myself, *Never forget how this looks.* I would replay the images over and over just to make sure I always had a mental photo of the vast beauty. I can still see purple lightning flashing across the South Dakota plains at four in the morning; humongous white, fluffy clouds spanning the entire sky in Montana; and lakes as clear as glass in Banff. All these things were so huge and screamed of the powers of an almighty Creator. Those massive forms inspire our insignificant human lives, and yet . . . God is subtle. He didn't reveal himself to me through a mountain moving or rivers parting but with an infinitesimal part of the Earth.

When thinking of a sixteen-year-old girl, most people imagine the stereotypical rebellious kid who dyes her hair, has tons of piercings, and likes to listen to music her parents hate, right? Girls like this sneak out and try illegal substances. They have fun and make mistakes and twenty years later tell other sixteen-year-olds not to do that. I'm pretty sure I am one of the few girls who ever took these testimonies to heart. I was the girl who listened to the adults and didn't feel the need to find out for myself. I was quiet, opinionated, smart, and adventurous (not in a risky way). I was the kid who never really talked back and always kept the other kids in line. I was the kid who made the honor roll, hung out with good kids, and didn't even know that marijuana and pot were the same thing. I was, simply put, very naive—and I liked it that way. I had no reason to complain; I loved my parents, and I loved where I was at.

However, as a sixteen-year-old girl, life was all about boys. All my friends were dating, my sister was dating, my cousins were dating . . . everyone was dating someone. For me, though, I was in this vortex where boys existed as fairy tales; you only talked to them if they wanted to borrow your pencil. I was not flirty; I wore modest clothes and was reserved. As the smart girl, I was told many times that I was too intimidating for boys to approach. At the same time, I observed the ways some other girls got boys' attention, and I knew I would never compromise like that. So I waited.

Waiting, though, is incredibly hard. After about two years, my life began to feel heavy. My sophomore year of high school was atrocious. I did not enjoy my classes, and I felt completely out of the loop socially. Being alone wasn't something I thought about every day, but it was this weight, a nagging feeling preying on my mind, which would surface occasionally and come out in tearful conversations with my mother. I would journal about my feelings, but I don't remember praying. At that time, it was too embarrassing to tell God what I was sad about. I knew it was silly; I didn't want him to feel my burden. It was trivial for such a big God—he was reserved for tragedies and grown-up problems.

So I stumbled on through these insecurities and feelings of being unwanted without much guidance or any answers. Canada hit, though, and my problem blew up. A lot of conversation with my cousins centered around boyfriends. Whenever I even heard the word mentioned, I would quickly turn the other way. It was already bad enough that no one wanted me, but I really didn't want my cousins to know I couldn't relate to their issues. As the week went on, more and more stories and situations arose to tear at the mask covering my insecurity.

I vividly remember the day my cousin Suzanna and I took a walk by our cabin to explore. We meandered toward a riverbank as she explained her situation with an ex-boyfriend. As I was listening to her tale, a voice of insecurity and depression whispered lies of my unworthiness. Tears began to well in my eyes as she finished her story and walked away. I quickly went the other direction just to gain a hold on my emotions. I couldn't believe I was so upset; I told myself to calm down but couldn't. So much despair rolled over me, and all I could think was, *I need to tell Mom.*

Telling Mom was my default; I told her whatever was on my mind. I remember being so upset that she wasn't right there with me to talk about it. As I stood there for a second, a new thought crept into my mind: *God could hear me too; he could hear me right at this very moment. He may actually care enough. I could tell him.* So with my new revelation, I decided to see if he could hear me. I stood there and silently poured out my innermost desires and desperation. I allowed myself to let a few tears escape, and in a moment my heart was a little more peaceful.

I turned to go find my cousin, and as I did, I looked down into the river. Right there, catching the light, was a little red stone in the shape of a heart. The water was quietly lapping against its side, and the magenta hue was the only color I could see for a moment. I numbly picked it up in disbelief. Was this from God, or was I being an idiot? I looked at this stone, with a perfect heart-shaped indent from the angle I had looked, and thought, *Could God really time something like that for me?* I kept holding the stone and turning it in my hand, thinking and praying and crying. I wiped my eyes and staggered over to my cousin. I smiled as she showed me something she had found, and then I silently walked back to the cabin with her.

Later that night, I sat and sobbed until I had no more tears. *What could this mean, Lord?* I didn't have a definite word . . . I just knew that he was with me. He was there to listen to me. And that always, no matter what, he would hold my hand. I hoped that it meant my time was coming and he had not forgotten my desire for love, but at the very least it was a promise and a new perspective on life. I could pray to God, and he would listen. I met my Savior again that day. My faith was truly reignited. I remember writing in my journal, "I don't know what this means. I'm ok with not knowing—I feel peaceful about it, and I'll wait on him." Four months later, he brought me the first stage in the fulfillment of his promise.

No one could ever reason out that experience and tell me that the Lord did not show up for me that day. I believe wholeheartedly that he spoke to me in a beautifully poetic way. I keep my stone close as a reminder of his promise, and I've learned that God truly does keep his promises. Waiting is crucial to his plan, but he knows when we're ready for what he has.

My time in Canada was irreplaceable. It took me getting away from my everyday life to see that God is bigger than my sadness.

Santa Fe

As we drove into Santa Fe that evening, the sky was still cloudy with occasional rain, but it didn't feel threatening anymore. It was just the welcome relief of a cool, soaking rain in the heat of a dry summer.

We spent the evening in Santa Fe, with a late-night dinner at one of the restaurants directly across from the old town square. Our meal included genuine blue-corn tortillas and honey-drizzled sopapillas Santa Fe–style (something you should not miss if you're ever there). We laughed and teased each other almost in the shadow of the oldest mission in the West, Chapel San Miguel, built between 1610 and 1625.

The next morning we made the forty-minute drive north to El Santuario de Chimayo. It was here that I'd experienced God's ability to work outside of my evangelical Christian comfort zone. Sometimes thought of as the "Lourdes of America," this shrine has been associated with miracles. On my previous visits I had encountered a God who could heal and transform lives with something as humble as the dirt from within the mission's walls.

It seemed fitting for us to come full circle. We had left Nashville in search of reconnecting as a family. We had hoped for a restoration of our love and trust, both in God and in each other. Paige and I had prayed for God to reveal himself to our kids—to help Bethany recover from last year's terrible ordeal, to win Jessica's trust, and to help Caleb grow into a young man. We had hoped for God to kindle in each of them a genuine passion and interest in the faith of Christianity and for them to enjoy some of God's beauty in Creation.

Those events all occurred. Our requests were fully met by God—those and so many more. I found that God was sparking in my kids and in me a deeper desire to explore the world, to engage different cultures, and to learn about new facets of his character, his heart, and his ways.

What started out as an unusual directive from God for how I could rebuild my disconnected, broken home had turned into an amazing lifetime memory of fourteen days in an SUV with my family. These two weeks had changed all of our lives.

I-40 Eastward to Home

After Santa Fe, the missions, and the beauty of the New Mexico mountains and desert, we turned our vehicle east and jumped back on Interstate 40 to return home. Saturday and Sunday were a blur. We discovered old Route 66 and the Big Texan Steakhouse in Amarillo, spent the night in Oklahoma City, and cruised through the Ozarks and Memphis, capturing sights and sounds as we drove through the heartland of the American South. We ate grits and BBQ with cole-slaw, downing countless cups of coffee and large sweet teas along the way. Our kids still argued and teased each other, but something profound had happened.

Their world was bigger now. Their view of life and death, history and culture, was no longer limited to a sixty-mile radius of their front door. They had begun to see the largeness of life, the possibilities for their future. They'd experienced beauty and danger, serenity and sadness; they'd felt the fatigue of endless days and the fear of a savage storm. They'd found the allure of the wilderness and the unspeakable beauty of a sunset on the Great Plains. They'd felt the rigors of a long and draining hike as well as the relief of a simple bed after a long day. In short, our kids had glimpsed the world as it is. Diminished was the urgent call of the world to speed up, catch up, and conquer all. They still had normal worries and fears, but gone was the ache of unnamed rejection and faithless love. Those things had been replaced by joy, by the contentment that comes from knowing that God is there, he does care, and he has a plan for each of our lives.

My kids had found their faith—not by my cunning plans to en-gage them emotionally and trick them into belief, but by genuinely feeling God's presence. Their hearts had been convicted by the simple and profound evidence of a beautiful God and a caring Savior. God had revealed himself to them in unique and powerful ways, reaching out to them where they were, offering a specific message of hope and love crafted for their hearts alone.

It's my hope that such faith will be brought into your home as well. How? Engage with God yourself and then listen to his custom-designed answers for your family's needs. If you do that, I believe with all my heart you will find the same God we did on our road trip to redemption.

ROAD-TRIP THEOLOGY: LEARNING TO READ THE ROAD SIGNS

The will of God will not take us where the grace of God cannot sustain us.

BILLY GRAHAM

REMEMBER THE METAPHOR we used way back at the beginning of the book? Parenting can be a lot like taking a long road trip. As moms and dads, we're trying so hard to keep our families safe and heading in the right direction that sometimes we forget we're not the ones in control of the car. We'll all face obstacles as we drive, and we have a choice in how to handle them: we can either react in fear, clutching the steering wheel ever more tightly, or we can react in trust, remembering that God is directing our way. But when it comes down to our day-to-day parenting choices, we have to move past the theoretical. What can we do to become safer "drivers" and make sure we're not standing in the way of the work God wants to do in our families?

I want to take a few minutes here to recap where we've been on our trip. I've summarized the thoughts and principles from the earlier chapters, distilling each chapter's message down to a few key lessons. My hope is that these spiritual "road signs" will be memorable enough to stick in your mind and help you the next time you're struggling. Think of these as the parenting equivalent of those big, orange signs you see on the highway. We zoom by them every day as we get from point A to point B and hardly notice them. Both in the real world and in the world of parenting, these signs are easy to ignore. But if we pay attention and respect their messages, they will help us travel the road wisely and safely.

Reading a book like this can generate all kinds of emotions. Some of you may feel as if you are way beyond the wisdom expressed in this book. Maybe you're well down the road of life and past the stage of raising teenagers. If that's the case, I'm grateful you cared enough to read our story. Please consider pouring your life wisdom into other families who are still navigating this season of life and working desperately to make sense of it all.

I suspect that far more of you may feel as if you're way behind. You may even worry that you've blown it too badly to ever recover. To that I say, "Balderdash." If I want you to get one thing from this book, it's the pivotal truth that our God is a redemptive and restorative God. He loves to fix stuff. You might say he's an expert at redemption; he can and does specialize in recovering everything lost or broken in our lives. If our story does nothing else, it should convince you of God's divine ability to repair and restore the messed-up pieces of broken lives. After all, he healed our family. He can heal yours, too.

Chapter One
YIELD TO THE HOLY SPIRIT

Seek wisdom from God as you interpret your child's behavior.

When we rely on our own ability to read our children's actions and attitudes, and when we respond to them solely out of our own limited understanding, we will crash and burn. We need to seek the Holy Spirit's leading and ask him to illuminate the reason behind our children's behavior.

NO BAGGAGE

Break free of the past—yours and your children's—and focus on the present.

It's so easy to make assumptions about our children's struggles and attitudes based on what has happened before. We get stuck in patterns of interacting and become blind to anything that doesn't fit the patterns. Because we think we know our kids, we cease to really see them. We need to focus on who they are now—not who they were two years ago or two months ago, and not who we think they might be in the future. We need to ask God for eyes to see clearly what is in front of us.

CAUTION—REDUCE SPEED

Look beyond the external behavior to the heart.

As parents, we all have the potential to overreact to our kids' behavior and miss the larger issues at hand. If we're not careful and intentional in our prayer life, we can easily overfocus on their external actions and underfocus on the condition of their hearts. This creates a serious risk of legalistically training them to withdraw their truest selves from our gaze. We need to ask God to prevent us from overreacting to outward actions and to give us insight into the heart issues underneath.

Chapter Two
SOUL CONSTRUCTION AHEAD

Let God change you first.

If we are going to succeed in raising our kids, in guiding or correcting them in any meaningful way, we need to accept that God will want to change us first. His principle of transformation almost always involves working with the leaders before he moves on to everyone else. In the parenting world, that means parents first, kids second. If we want to see real changes in our kids and our marriages, we must grow beyond the stagnant patterns of our personal comfort and convenience.

DETOUR AROUND FEAR

Be motivated by love, not fear.

To help our children grow to love and follow God for a lifetime, first we have to back away from our predisposition to live out of fear and learn to follow Christ out of love. Fear is not a healthy way to raise families. It forces us to behave frantically whenever things start to feel out of our control. When fear rules us, we are actually stepping out of our God-given role as parents and beginning to play God in our kids' lives. That kind of approach will mess things up for them and for us.

Learning to follow Christ out of love will change every dynamic of our lives. This motivational shift is essential if we are ever going to grow beyond a cyclical pattern of fear and regret. When fear rules, peace will not be present in our families. Children can see through our carefully constructed Christian masks to the insecure people we really are. Only when we truly accept the love of Christ will we be able to let go of our need to be in charge.

Chapter Three
PROCEED WITH GRACE

Develop a deep understanding of grace, and reject the guilt that comes from "earned faith."

To successfully move forward with your kids, you will need to reconcile with your past. No baggage is healthy, especially when we drag it into our families' lives. For many of us, that baggage is a deep history of living with guilt as the crux of our relationship with God. Believing in "earned faith" at any level will corrupt the pure strength of the gospel, leaving us heavily burdened with guilt when things go wrong. We must embrace grace wholeheartedly, admitting that we can do nothing to earn it.

NO "LONE RANGER" PARENTING

Seek unity in your marriage and your parenting.

Marriage and parenting require unity to succeed. When one parent is isolated from the other, you sabotage your ability to accurately understand and respond to your kids' needs. If one parent with a dominant personality crowds out the influence of the other, you're in great danger of making some huge mistakes.

God's design for parenting includes a team: a husband and a wife.

If you disrupt that design and substitute your own, it will have disastrous consequences. If you are a single parent, your need for counsel and assistance is greatly increased, and you should seek wisdom from God and from your community of faith. To fill this gap, prayerfully consider allowing a family friend to play a larger role in giving your child the support and encouragement that would normally come from a second parent.

PRAYER ZONE

Devote yourselves to prayer.

For parents, praying over and for your family is not an optional exercise. Only through prayer and time in the Word can the Holy Spirit guide us to the best ways to reach our kids.

Chapter Four
STOP FAKING IT

Don't be satisfied with behavior modification in your kids.
Seek heart transformation.

Behavior modification does not produce authentic faith. Outward disciplines without inward change create cynical and disingenuous adults. Instead, our goal is to introduce our children to the immeasurable love of God and then let him do the work of transforming their lives.

JUNCTION AHEAD

Demonstrate love to your kids through spending time with them.

To effectively transfer faith from one generation to another, parents must demonstrate genuine love to their kids. Time is the universal language of love. When we say we love our kids but are too busy for them, we become hypocrites. If that trend is not changed, we will undermine our parenting messages of faith and weaken our children's respect for and trust in God. Seek ways to reconnect with your kids, and make family time a true priority in your schedule.

MERGE REAL FAITH WITH REAL LIFE

Be authentic. Model for your kids what a real—not perfect—relationship with God can look like.

Authenticity is nonnegotiable if we wish to see our children embrace our faith. We all know what it means to live two separate lives. If our Sunday faith doesn't affect our Monday behavior, then we have a problem. Living authentically does not mean being a perfect Christian example to our kids, but it does require us to respond to their criticisms honestly and admit when we mess up.

* * *

God's path for your family may be significantly different from anyone else's. And that's okay. Resist the urge to pattern your family after someone else's.

Remember, formulas will not work in the long term. Neither will reliance on our own plans and preparation. We must find our source of wisdom and strength in the promises of God's Word, not in the confidence of our own understanding. God has designed a divine strategy, a customized road map for every family, and it is essential that we discover it for ourselves and apply its insights to our kids.

No matter how dark or difficult the family situation we're facing, we need to hold on to the promise that God is working and that he can do more than we ever dreamed—for his honor and glory. When you're discouraged, keep this verse at the forefront of your mind: "Now to him who is able to do far more abundantly than all that we ask or think, according to the power at work within us, to him be glory in the church and in Christ Jesus throughout all generations, forever and ever. Amen" (Ephesians 3:20-21, ESV).

May God richly bless you . . . as we all seek to keep our families safe on the road to true life.

Paige's Story

My Reflections on Our Journey

I AM A NATURAL OBSERVER—one who loves to watch my family enjoying themselves and experiencing new, awe-inspiring things. That's how it was for me in Canada and the many states through which we traveled. I often stood back and watched as my kids interacted with their beloved cousins, their grandparents, and especially their dad. After all we've been through, I will never forget that the unity of our family is a miracle, so I inwardly rejoice any time I get to witness them all having fun, seeing amazing sights, taking in the nature around them, and getting excited about life. On our trip I tried to catch as many of those moments as I could on my camera, often taking a shot from a distance to capture all the beauty, as well as my family's joy at seeing it.

As a mom, I have always sought out moments with my children that I can store in my memory and keep for a lifetime. This trip was no different.

My favorite memory with Caleb was when we were simply standing by a beautiful, swiftly moving stream in the Canadian Rockies. All around us were small bunches of pink and purple wildflowers. He and I watched the water, threw in rocks, and practiced taking close-up photos of the blooms. We walked a bit farther to a railroad track that seemed to go on forever. My choice to spend time with him at that moment is a forever memory that I can remember without even looking at the pictures.

With Jessica and Bethany, my best memory is persevering together to get to the rustic but quaint Lake Agnes Tea House. Before we could enjoy the gorgeous view, we had to hike about two miles—straight uphill. On the way there we moaned and groaned, challenging each other to keep going on the seemingly never-ending trail. But once we arrived, our strenuous effort was overshadowed by us girls being able to sit down and drink hot tea served from a pewter teapot. We got so excited about the foods we could choose: peanut butter and jelly on hearty whole-grain bread, pimento cheese on raisin bread, and different flavors of scones. During our exhausting climb, we never could have imagined that *this* was what awaited us.

As I write this more than two years later, I can see that the hike to the teahouse sums up our story: taking the long way up—even with all the bumps, curves, and extreme frustrations—can get you to something that you will never forget and that you never imagined was possible. Two years ago, I wouldn't have believed that our family would come through the months of anguish not only intact but closer than before. I never would have envisioned Bethany as a young woman who is characterized not by her struggles but instead by her love for God. Today she is an example to me of walking through life with peace. On her dresser mirror she posts Scripture and words of encouragement that remind her of who she is in Christ; that's her identity now, unlike the darkness and negativity that used to so greatly define her. She has become "softer," with herself and with those around her. It is a reflection of what she has allowed God to do for her, and she extends that grace to others. She is waiting patiently on God to lead her to the right college.

Two years ago, I couldn't have foreseen the intense pride we would feel when Jessica graduated from high school and then began her college adventure with courage and independence. She has even surprised herself, saying that she can't believe how outgoing she has become—in direct contrast to the timid girl who never saw herself as someone who could carry on a conversation and was so fearful to try. Today she seeks out new adventures: preparing for a spring break mission trip to Panama City, Florida, taking an Arabic class that doesn't give her school credit but just piqued her interest, signing up to model for a "love your body" fashion show, and loving dorm life because of all the new people she gets to meet. In ways that only he could, God guided her to the perfect college, where she has begun the journey of discovering his plan for her life and who he created her to be.

Caleb is fifteen and a sophomore in high school. He misses Jessica when she's away at college; however, he and Bethany have become closer than I could have predicted years ago. They still get on each other's nerves, but their times of conversation and laughter now outweigh their arguments. Caleb is an outstanding artist, and I am grateful for his visual communications teacher, who is letting him explore his talent and grow in confidence.

Finally, I'm thankful for the growth in my marriage. During our time of crisis, I never dreamed that Brad and I would be sharing our story in book form—or that our pain might be used by God to help someone else who is struggling. But through God's grace, our incredible road trip and the experiences surrounding it have changed and healed our entire family. What seemed impossible to us became reality when we stepped back and watched our amazing, loving, trustworthy God at work.

Appendix

Planning Your Family's Road Trip

IF YOU'RE CONSIDERING PLANNING your own family road trip, you'll want to take some time to think through the details. Here are a few practical tips and ideas to help get you started.

The Rubber Meets the Road

Budget

Planning a trip takes time and energy. I recommend that you carefully plan a budget ahead of time so the critical emotional and mental focus you will need to connect with your kids isn't spent worrying about how much to spend on lunch.

On our trip with five people, we spent about $350 to $450 on long travel days, due to high gas costs, and closer to $300 to $350 on days when we stayed in one place.

We generally budgeted about $100 per day for miscellaneous fun stuff (go-karts, tours, canoeing, souvenirs, etc.) and about $30 per person for meals. This amount increased on travel days, as we ate out more when we were on the road. Part of the fun of traveling is eating out, and we always took the extra money along knowing that when we "tortured" our kids with twelve-plus-hour driving days, we should at least provide them with some eating-out rewards along the way. Also look at your vehicle's gas mileage to estimate how much gas will cost.

Most of the time, you can grab a hotel on Priceline.com for $75 to $80 in any region. However, an average family like ours has three kids and two adults, and that may create some stress with hotel rooms that are set up with two double beds. We tried to call ahead and get a fold-out couch for as many stops as possible, but some cities have very strict fire codes and will not allow five in a hotel room at all. Be aware of that potential glitch in your budgets and planning.

For the kids' spending money, we planned way ahead and had them save up allowances, earn some extra money babysitting, and sell some of their old stuff on eBay and at a garage sale before we left. We also gave each of the kids about $150 cash for their own special purchases along the way, and we made it clear that we were not to be pestered with repeated requests for tourist-shop treasures. They would have to decide how they wanted to spend the money as we went. This arrangement worked very well.

My brother and his family packed some sandwich ingredients, and we did eat a couple of meals picnic-style as we traveled to Canada. In retrospect, it was very difficult to get everything out and prepared with so much luggage in the van and SUV. Next time, to save costs and time on the heavy travel days, I would bring a smaller cooler and eat sandwiches for lunch as we drove, but have a quick breakfast at the hotel and a drive-through dinner.

Once you arrive at your destination, plan to buy some simple food for breakfast or lunch and eat out just one meal a day. This will really cut costs down. You may even find you have more money left over for special excursions. There will always be lots to do, and hardly anything will be free. Planning realistically for the costs of a road trip will help reduce family/spousal stress. The whole point is to have a great time together, so why not do everything possible to keep the friction to a minimum? Reducing the known stress factors will help immensely; believe me, enough unknown ones will pop up on their own.

Other Factors

Unplugging the electronics and combating the insatiable need for stimulation will make the first two days of travel very challenging for most teens. Some families may need to consider a bit of a transitional truce, with a few hours of "unplugged" time alternating with "plugged" time. Reaching some destinations may take many hours or days of travel, and it may not be realistic to try to pull your kids off their daily doses of electronic medication all at once.

Pray about each day before you start out, asking God to protect you. Also ask him to help you remain patient and to give you wisdom to defuse any altercations you might have among family members. It's critical that you as the parent do not give in to the temptation to vent on your kids too much. Set the tone and the example. If and when you blow it, just apologize and model the process of forgiveness and reconciliation. Be ready to both give grace to your kids and receive it from them.

A family road trip doesn't have to be huge. Weekends work too! Great reconnecting for a family can occur with short trips to local state or national parks near your home. Just pick a spot, get out, and get moving.

Final Road-Trip Considerations

Not all families will have the time or resources just to jump in the car and speed off to find happiness. That's not the point. Be sure to pray intentionally about God's solution for your family. If you sense it's time to take a road trip like ours, that's great. But carefully consider the when, where, and how factors before launching right in.

Weeks and months of parenting prayer should cover this event before you go. Rely completely on the Holy Spirit to prepare each person's heart and mind. Understand the need for God to orchestrate the timing, context, and content of the messages essential for each individual member of your family. Don't panic if you feel inadequate to speak with your teens about life issues or a painful past. You are not alone. Jesus himself will be with you; his timing is perfect, his words complete.

When you have the time, place, and plan confirmed, commit to it—and hold fast to your plan no matter what. You will find that every possible distraction, delay, and reason to cancel your time with your family will arise, often most intensely right before you leave. Marriages will be attacked, trust undermined, and finances drained. Work will amp up like never before. There is an enemy behind all these obstacles. When it's clear that we as parents have made the spiritual commitment to help our families reconnect and heal, the devil will unleash everything possible to prevent us from following through on the divinely inspired strategies we will be given for touching our kids' hearts.

In the end, we must rely on God's grace to win our kids to the Christian worldview. Not one of us can handle the task of bringing our kids safely from childhood to adulthood without God's help. Obviously that starts with our personal relationship with God and his Word, but that truth should also translate into our interpersonal lives. Walking out our spiritual struggles with trusted friends and connecting with our local communities of faith are essential anchors for the modern-day family.

Just taking a road trip will not solve all—or maybe any—of the problems you currently have. But I guarantee you it will help you reconnect and rekindle the most important relationships we will ever be given.

Reflecting on our two-week family road trip, I can honestly say that it was the greatest adventure of my life so far. I'm already looking forward to the next one. Soon it will be time for me to hit the road again. I can hear the mountains softly calling to me. . . . Can you?

With genuine love and appreciation,
Brad

For bonus *Road Trip to Redemption* content, including a travel plan of the Mathias family's journey, scan the QR code or visit www.tyndal.es/RoadTripBonus.

Notes on Chapter Opener Photos

Endnotes

1. A. W. Tozer, *The Knowledge of the Holy* (San Francisco: Harper–San Francisco, 1992), 3.
2. Drew Dyck, "The Leavers: Young Doubters Exit the Church," *Christianity Today*, November 19, 2010, http://www.christianitytoday.com/ct/2010/november/27.40.html?paging=off.
3. Brian Hardin, *Passages: How Reading the Bible in a Year Will Change Everything for You* (Grand Rapids, MI: Zondervan, 2011), 70.
4. The Barna Group, "Survey Describes the Ups and Downs of Tween Life," http://www.barna.org/barna-update/article/15-familykids/146-survey-describes-the-ups-and-downs-of-tween-life.
5. C. S. Lewis, *Mere Christianity* (New York: Macmillan, 1952), 68.
6. Peter Greig, *The Vision and the Vow* (Orlando, FL: Relevant Books, 2004), 119–122.
7. *Banff, Jasper & Glacier National Parks* (Victoria, Canada: Lonely Planet Publications, 2008), 109.
8. A. W. Tozer, *God's Pursuit of Man* (Camp Hill, PA: Wingspread Publishers, 2007), 13. Originally published as *The Divine Conquest* (Christian Publications, 1950).

About the Author

BRAD MATHIAS is president of Bema Media LLC, the parent company of iShine, the world's largest preteen Christian media group. He also serves as copastor of the Four Winds Anglican Mission in Spring Hill, Tennessee. Survivors of an almost-divorce, Brad and his wife, Paige, have been married for over twenty-two years and are the parents of three teenagers. Blessed with a redeemed marriage and a restored home, Brad is actively engaged in public ministry to families in crisis. At his blog, RoadTripParenting.com, Brad shares from his life experiences as a pastor, husband, father, and Christian media executive. An ardent outdoorsman, adventurer, and lifelong fan of road-tripping, Brad loves to explore hidden country trails and roads less traveled. Through his unique background and personal testimony, Brad provides an insightful and practical perspective on the challenges of modern-day parenting and family life.

Online Discussion *guide*

TAKE *your* TYNDALE READING EXPERIENCE *to the* NEXT LEVEL

A FREE discussion guide for this book is available at bookclubhub.net, perfect for sparking conversations in your book group or for digging deeper into the text on your own.

www.bookclubhub.net

You'll also find free discussion guides for other Tyndale books, e-newsletters, e-mail devotionals, virtual book tours, and more!

> RAISING YOUR KIDS
> TO BECOME
> SPIRITUAL CHAMPIONS

GEORGE BARNA

WHAT THE RESEARCH
SHOWS REALLY WORKS

revolutionary PARENTING

How can parents make a lasting impact in the spiritual lives of their children? To find the answer, George Barna researched the lives of thriving adult Christians and discovered the essential steps their parents took to shape their spiritual lives in childhood. He also learned surprising truths about which popular parenting tactics just aren't working. *Revolutionary Parenting* goes beyond youth group and Sunday school and shows parents how to instill in their children a vibrant commitment to Christ.

CP0289

Spiritual, life-changing content *by* Christian teens, *for* today's tweens.

iShine is a unique ministry dedicated to helping tweens develop faith that will last a lifetime as they find their value, identity, and purpose in Christ. iShine reaches tweens, families, and churches through resources like

- *iShine KNECT*—the #1 highest-rated Christian tween television program in the world (now in its fourth season!)
- Music videos and CDs, as well as online streaming of Christian and family-friendly hit music
- Live events and festivals: high-energy, biblically-based live performances with uplifting messages, multimedia interactive projection, and state-of-the art effects—performed by today's top teen artists
- Multimedia Christian preteen curriculum and resources for churches
- iShinelive.com offers daily Bible verses, games, *KNECT* TV episodes on demand, online chat, online prayer forum, and resources for parents and pastors.
- Social media: Find and follow iShine on 🐦 Twitter and 📘 Facebook!
- And much more!

To check out this amazing ministry, visit www.iShinelive.com. CP0587